Parenting the Millennial Generation

Parenting the Millennial Generation

Guiding Our Children Born between 1982 and 2000

Dave Verhaagen

Westport, Connecticut
London

Library of Congress Cataloging-in-Publication Data

Verhaagen, David Allan.
  Parenting the millennial generation : guiding our children born between
1982 and 2000 / Dave Verhaagen.
    p. cm.
  Includes bibliographical references and index.
  ISBN 0-275-98474-5 (alk. paper)
  1. Parenting—United States. 2. Generation Y—United States.
  3. Children—United States. 4. Teenagers—United States.
  5. Young adults—United States. I. Title.
  HQ755.8.V47 2005
  649'.1—dc22   2005018685

British Library Cataloguing in Publication Data is available.

Library of Congress Catalog Card Number: 2005018685
ISBN: 0-275-98474-5

First publised in 2005

Praeger Publishers, 88 Post Road West, Westport, CT 06881
An imprint of Greenwood Publishing Group, Inc.
www.praeger.com

Printed in the United States of America

The paper used in this book complies with the
Permanent Paper Standard issued by the National
Information Standards Organization (Z39.48-1984).

10 9 8 7 6 5 4 3 2 1

This book is dedicated to Ann and Herb Verhaagen,
my terrific parents who are now awesome grandparents

Contents

Acknowledgments

I've written a few other books, but they have all been co-authored with someone else. I discovered that writing a book all by myself is (shockingly) *double the work!* However, even though I say I wrote this on my own, it is really the product of a lot of collaboration.

My wife, Ellen, is an amazing mother and spouse. She loves our family well and models what it looks like to be a good parent every single day. She also made extensive edits to this manuscript that kept making it better. To say I'm grateful to her is a huge understatement.

Frank Gaskill, Jonathan Feather, and my other colleagues at Southeast Psychological Services are not only fun and cool people, but are also among the best in the field. They sharpened my thoughts, helped with the research, and gave me tremendous feedback throughout this process.

Drew Wozniak has been my research assistant for the past couple of years and has helped me out tremendously. He has a great mind and a love for learning that I admire greatly.

Finally, I am extremely grateful to the parents and kids I have met over the past few years who provided me with stories and insights. Without them, this book would be dry as dust. Their stories weave a richness into the text that will benefit many families for years to come.

Thanks to all of you.

INTRODUCTION

On Sunday April 18, 2004, a bus full of teenage soccer players from North Carolina sped down a rain-slick road just east of Paris, France. They were heading to the airport after ten days of matches that were part of the Olympic Development Program, which identifies and grooms the best young soccer players. "We're going too fast," a few of the guys thought, but no one said out loud; they assumed the driver knew what he was doing. As the bus flew around a curve near the town of Mitry-Mory, it began to tip over. Some of the boys remember it in slow motion. One of them grabbed at a bar, but most of the others were slammed against the inside of the bus as it crashed on its side with an explosive thud. It began to slide across the road with a sickening sound of grinding glass and metal.

One of the boys, Nick, had his arm trapped between the bus and the pavement. When the bus stopped sliding, his hand and arm were mangled. One of his friends was killed immediately. Another of his friends had severe injuries and died a few days later. Several others were injured. It was a gruesome and tragic event.

Nick was to endure several operations and a prolonged, frustrating stay in a French hospital. He continuously thought of his two friends who had died, one of whom he had known for years. When he returned to the United States, he faced painful physical therapy and still more operations. On top of this, he faced the loss of a dream. He had been on his way to being one of the best soccer players in the state, perhaps the country. Now it looked like it was all gone.

Such an event can destroy a person. Many would get discouraged and give up. Nick didn't even consider giving up. He worked hard during physical therapy, he returned to school and kept his grades up, and he even began training again. Within eight months of the accident, he was back on the soccer team, playing as well as ever.

His parents wanted him to talk with a therapist to make sure that he was okay emotionally. That's when I met him. What struck me was that even though the whole ordeal was traumatic and he had experienced great loss, he didn't let it hold him back. He dealt with it and moved on. He wasn't in denial; he felt sadness over the death of his friends and anger at the bus driver and the tour company. Yet he had no symptoms of post-traumatic stress or depression. We met several times only because we had good rapport and he valued our relationship, not because he had any deep emotional problems. He was the picture of good mental health. More than that, he was the model of a resilient child.

Today, Nick plays soccer, does well in school, has a girlfriend, and enjoys a good relationship with his parents. He took the worst that life could throw at him and he came out stronger. How did he do it? By the end of the book, you'll know.

Dozens of studies shaped this book. Research conducted at our practice with several hundred children and teens contributed greatly. Sprinkled throughout are accounts of my own experiences as both a child psychologist and a father. In the stories from my clinical practice, I've changed details such as names, physical descriptions, and specific facts to protect confidentiality. The one exception to this is Nick's story. His name really is Nick and all the details are just as they happened. He wanted his story told and I'm glad to do it.

I also share experiences from my own life from childhood to the present day. My intent is not to be self-indulgent; rather, I hope to be honest and to help you make a personal connection with this material that goes beyond research and facts.

I have much to share with you. I'll introduce you to this new generation of children, discuss the cultural context that has shaped their collective identity, talk about the qualities of an awesome parent, alert you to dangers and risks, and then spend a lot of time outlining what you can do to improve the lives of your children. It's a lot of ground to cover. Let's get going.

1

Who Is This Millennial Generation?

A mom sat across from me in my office, her brow knitted in concern for her son. He was a twelve-year-old kid who was failing school and looked likely to repeat the sixth grade. Worse still, he was completely defiant and belligerent at home. He refused to follow the simplest direction and would cuss her out at the slightest provocation. I agreed that things looked bad for her son, but I was optimistic there was a fighting chance of getting him back on track.

She asked me, "Do you see many kids like this?"

"I see kids like him every day," I said. "That's my job."

She looked puzzled for a moment; then she said, "What's wrong with kids today? Why do they act like this?"

I must admit that when all day long you see kids with problems it can give you the impression that today's youth is in a world of trouble. Many people have argued—some passionately so—that children and teens are worse than ever. We hear that they are ruder, more disrespectful, lazier, and even more violent than in the past. Other people have argued that it isn't the kids who have changed, but the entire culture that has shifted right under our feet. To them it seems we live in a different world than when we were kids. So which is it—different kids or a different world?

These questions have sent me on an exploration of the youth we are raising in today's culture. For more than a decade, I have interacted with this new generation. I want to understand them better, as I know you do. These are our kids, but they are very different from us and they've grown up in a different world. So here's the question: Does this generation of kids need a new approach to parenting? My answer is a decisive yes. This book will lay the groundwork for understanding these kids, their culture, and a parent's response to both.

A NEW GENERATION BREWING

A fascinating scene unfolds at a busy coffeehouse in the middle of town. It's a summer night, a nice breeze sweeping through the patio, some live jazz over in the courtyard. This is a good night to be out people-watching, I think to myself. There are some middle-aged folks chatting and one older couple reading together. A group of teenagers gathers out front. The boys have either chin-length hair or close-shaved heads, and they are all wearing baggy pants big enough to fit two people inside. A couple of the boys have skateboards under their arms. Their appearance reminds me of the hippies of the 1960s, yet their conversation is void of any high-minded idealism. And unlike the previous generation, they seem light-years from angst. Peals of laughter erupt often from the group and most of them seem to be smiling and having fun. These are happy kids. It's a refreshing sight to watch.

Meet the Millennial Generation. They are individuals born between the year Reagan took office and the beginning of the new millennium. They have no memory of a time before MTV. They are 72 million strong, the biggest generation in U.S. history, surpassing even the Baby Boomer generation in size.

Unlike Generation X (kids born in the 1960s and 1970s), which was initially elusive and hard to define, the Millennials have already begun to form a generational identity. They are already beginning to have an impact on our culture. Some social commentators have already said that this generation will likely have a positive impact well into the twenty-first century. However, as with all generations, there is good news and bad news about the kind of change they are bringing.

I'VE GOT SOME GOOD NEWS . . .

When Generation X was growing up during the 1970s and 1980s, the cultural focus was on adults and their individual rights. Parents felt free to divorce and to follow their own pursuits. Even within intact families, children often had to fend for themselves. The term "latchkey child" was coined during the childhood of Generation X. During this sad era, children were often implicitly viewed as barriers to adult fulfillment.

So the Millennials arrived just as we realized what a mess we were making of our children. This new crop of infants rode in minivans with "Baby on Board" signs, driven by parents who pushed children's issues to the forefront of the social debate. Child abuse and child safety became political campaign issues. Other topics, such as tax cuts and program funding, became framed in terms of their effects on children and families. William Bennett's *The Book of Virtues* topped the bestseller lists and spawned a rash of similar books with a family-values theme.

The shift back to a focus on children began toward the end of the 1980s and is continuing. This correction takes many forms: tax breaks for families with children, reforms in adoption and foster care legislation, "family-friendly" restaurants and other businesses, huge increases in the sales of children's videos, national dialogue about protecting children from adult content in the media, tightening of youth curfews in many localities, sweeping reforms in the juvenile justice codes in most states, and so on.

In short, our culture has come to care for its children once again. Whereas the Xers have been called the "Repair Generation" because they had to clean up after the self-indulgent parties of the previous generation, the Millennials are the heirs to a culture that has finally come back to its senses. Children are once again rightly viewed as special and in need of guidance, nurturance, and limits. As a whole, they appear to have much healthier, happier childhoods than their Generation X counterparts. Consequently, they are not saddled with the relational dysfunction that has typified Generation X. The Millennials are a well-nurtured, well-connected generation.

Family

The Millennials are as family oriented as any generation before them. Three-quarters of them say they get along well—if not *extremely* well—with their parents. Shockingly, only 3 percent report not getting along well with their parents. Nearly half of them say a family member is their top role model and claim they would spend more time with their family if they could. One of my clients, a seventeen-year-old football player, told me recently that the highlight of his weekend was playing board games with his family. I had a hard time picturing this burly guy playing Parcheesi, but I knew he was telling me the truth.

According to the social researcher George Barna, fully nine out of ten Millennials consider their family "healthy and functional." Whether this is objectively true or not is another matter; the point here is that these kids have a positive view of their families. They see family as important and desirable. When I ask the teenagers I see at my office about the most important things in their lives, family is almost always near the top of the list. As one boy recently told me, "I just want to get along with my parents. I can't stand it when we argue. Having a good relationship with them is my biggest goal right now." Yes, family matters to this generation of kids.

Race

The Millennials are also the most racially diverse generation in U.S. history. Over one-third of this generation is African-American or Hispanic. By the year 2050, the current "minorities" will be the majority of our population. The face of the nation is changing, and it is becoming darker. In many schools, racial issues are discussed and confronted directly in ways that were not imaginable even twenty years ago. Although nearly a quarter of African-American teenagers report being victimized because of their race, a large poll conducted in 2003 found that 89 percent of African-American teenagers considered racism only "a small problem" or "not a problem at all" in their personal lives. More children and adolescents report having friendships with those of other races than ever before. This is especially good news for those of us who have long worked for racial reconciliation.

Technology

The Millennials are also a technologically sophisticated generation. Their world has always had computers and compact discs. Vinyl albums, eight-track tapes, and Atari video games are amusing relics to them. Now, the majority of all households in the United States with children aged seven years or younger have personal computers. The Millennials are so technology savvy they make the Xers look almost computer illiterate. Their ability to use computer applications, navigate the Internet, and use other personal technologies is astounding. I once observed three high school seniors carry on a conversation with each other while one was playing a video game and the other two were text messaging each other in a parallel conversation. It was fascinating to watch, but it reinforced how much the use of technology had become second nature to them. Half of the teens surveyed in a 2003 poll of 1,000 students across the country said that they are interested in pursuing a career in a technology field. In an increasingly technology-centered culture, these young people are well positioned to take us far into the twenty-first century.

Academics

This is probably the most academic, achievement-oriented generation that our country has ever seen. The majority of high school seniors plan to go to college, and they are serious about it. They get good grades, take SAT prep classes, do community service, and grab leadership roles when they can.

It has never been as competitive to get into college as it is now, but these Millennials have stepped up to bat academically. Gone are the days when a mediocre student could waltz into a decent state university. Many college admissions officers will tell you they've never seen applications such as these, representing such a high caliber of students.

This academic intensity can cause them trouble, though. In 2003, 80 percent of students said that the pressure to get good grades is a problem for them, up 16 percent from two years earlier. The pressure is increasing, and they are feeling it. This is true not just of teenagers; younger kids are feeling it, too. One girl told me, "I have a lot of homework, but it's worth it because I want to go to a really good college." She was eleven years old. These Millennials are academic, achievement-oriented kids who take school seriously—perhaps too seriously at times.

Music

Popular music is a great barometer of a generation's mood and of its attitude toward life. Think about the Baby Boomers and you recall any number of bands at Woodstock, full of righteous indignation and idealistic zeal. Think about the Xers and you imagine Kurt Cobain and the grunge rockers, full of self-loathing and troubled introspection. But think about the Millennials and you already think about a new breed of young performers, full of a carefree optimism and upbeat outlooks.

Hanson, a musical trio of teenage brothers, exploded onto the scene in the early days of this generation with their first CD, which sold well over 6 million copies. It was the definition of bubblegum pop, with its signature song, "MMMBop," imploring us to hold onto our friends. When speaking of his angst-filled predecessors, lead singer and keyboardist Taylor Hanson wondered, "If music is what you do, and you love it, why would you be sad?" Echoing that sentiment is the superbly talented teenage blues guitarist Jonny Lang, who said, "For me it's like a big myth, I think, that you have to lead this huge life of misery and be down on your luck constantly to play the kind of music that I play. . . . I'm always really happy. Is that wrong?"

Whether it's Hillary Duff for younger kids or John Mayer for the older ones, performers are increasingly positive. Having such optimistic messengers across the musical spectrum is an especially good development. According to Howe and Strauss, "The more positive the pop-culture role models, the better." This is unquestionably true. Teenage musicians such as these, along with their young counterparts in acting and sports, will have a profound influence on what this generation believes to be right or wrong, acceptable or unacceptable.

Without question, there are some Millennials who gravitate toward music with dark or morbid themes, but they are in the minority. Even in alternative musical genres, lyrics tend to be more optimistic than in the past. Most Millennials seem to enjoy music that is lighter and more hopeful about life.

Politics

The Millennials are already more politically conscious than the Xers were at the same age. Scores of young Millennials lobby local, state, and federal governments to take political action. They are hopeful that government and other institutions can be used for positive means.

For example, when Suellen Adams's fourth and fifth grade class learned that the hundred-year-old mother of their school custodian had been denied citizenship because of misfiled paperwork, they decided to do something about it. They wrote dozens of letters to Congress lobbying on behalf of the Chinese centenarian, Oai Banh. Two months later, Banh was given her citizenship in a ceremony in their school, Martha Lake Elementary, with her family and her new young friends surrounding her. This is just one example of Millennials jumping into the political process.

Success

Everyone wants to have a successful life, but how someone defines success tells us much about that person—and about a generation. Earlier generations defined success as achieving the American Dream of a good job, a house, two kids, and all the comforts. Not long ago, the Baby Boomers defined success as making an impact on their world. So how do the Millennials define success? In a survey of more than 1,000 teens, their top five definitions of success were

1. Personal satisfaction with what you are doing
2. Having close family relationships
3. Having a close group of friends
4. Having an active religious/spiritual life
5. Making a contribution to society

Not a bad list! Although the Boomer ideal got demoted to fifth place, the concepts here are very healthy. Notice the themes of relationship—with self, family, friends, God, and community. Less than a third said success was defined by making lots of money; less than a quarter said it was defined by being famous; less than a tenth said it was being attractive or popular. This is a healthy group with a mature, highly relational view of life's meaning.

* * *

The Millennials have arrived as a family-oriented, diverse, well-nurtured, high-achieving, technologically savvy, and socially minded generation.

They have energy and a collective sense of generational identity that is refreshing and good. As a generation, they don't seem to mind being upbeat and positive. Optimism has become cool once again.

. . . AND I HAVE SOME BAD NEWS

Even with all this good news, there are some significant concerns about the Millennials. The first bit of bad news has to do with the true condition of the family. Although the culture recognizes the need for strong parenting, the reality is that the number of fatherless families is on the rise. Nearly a majority of Millennials will spend all or part of their childhood without a father in the home. Some estimates suggest that as many as 55 percent will live with only their mother; this is currently equivalent to more than 12 million single-parent families in the United States.

Another sobering reality is that the gap between the "haves" and the "have-nots" among families is widening. A full 25 percent of children under the age of six are currently living at or below poverty level, which is defined as an annual income of less than $15,141 for a family of four.

We must look, too, at the downside of the technological sophistication of this generation. Because of the Internet, cable, and video stores, children are exposed to adult content at increasingly early ages. These technologies, coupled with the shifting morality of today's culture, make it easy for young people to hear and see things that have traditionally been reserved for adults. Children can easily view hardcore pornography via the Internet. Many children watch graphically violent films and discuss them at school, often to the dismay of their teachers. Several years ago, a chill ran through me as a nine-year-old boy gleefully told me about a movie he had seen the night before where one man got shot in the head and another got his arm shot off.

In addition to seeing violent movies, children frequently hear discussions of such adult topics as abortion, homosexuality, and marital infidelity. We initiate our children into adulthood at increasingly early ages. This has enormous implications for how our kids will think about social and moral issues in the future. Being numbed by violence, eroticized by pornography, and jaded by adult conversations may have poisonous impact, especially for the most vulnerable kids.

Here are other unsettling facts about the behavior of this generation. Nearly 2 million adolescents have at least five alcoholic drinks every week. Although the overall rates of illegal drug use are declining, twice the number of adolescents use hallucinogens at least once a month as in the

1980s. Every day another 3,000 children start smoking, 1,000 underage girls give birth, 48 adolescents contract the HIV virus, and 15 children and teenagers die in gun-related incidents. The Millennials' world has always included AIDS and drive-by shootings—things that did not even exist during the childhoods of other generations. Many counselors report that date violence among adolescents is also on the increase.

So there you have it: the good, the bad, and the ugly. If we can bring it all together, what does a composite picture of the Millennial generation look like?

SO, WHAT ABOUT KIDS THESE DAYS?

This generation of kids is terrific from top to bottom, despite the challenges. From the oldest to the youngest among them, they are all part of a generation that will make a profound and positive impact on our culture. They are terrific fun, with their sharp, sarcastic wit and their playfulness. Most of them love their parents and are loyal to their friends. They work hard in school—much harder than most of us ever did—and are highly competitive over sports and grades and college acceptance. They are a truly great group.

Shepherd Smith, founder and president of the Institute for Youth Development, says, "This generation of adolescents is shaping up to be the best this country has seen in decades and it's reason for every American to be thankful." I agree with him wholeheartedly. Although many people are fond of saying "kids are worse today than ever," the facts don't line up with this assessment. Again, Mr. Smith says

When it comes to making decisions and choices about their behavior, today's teens are wiser than those of yesterday. Indeed, the main thing that teenagers are rebelling against today seems to be rebellious behavior itself. Teen sex is down, school violence is down, and even smoking among teens is starting to decline. Two-thirds of today's teenagers report that faith in God is an important part of their life and rank values as very important, as well. This may be a great generation in the making.

His assertions are right on the money, entirely supported by solid research and plenty of evidence.

Back in 1991, when it was fashionable to lament the condition of our youth, Howe and Straus, the great generational researchers and thinkers, predicted, "around the year 2000, America's news weeklies will run cover stories singing the praise of American youth." Boy, were they right. *Time* was about two months early, showcasing a positive feature entitled

"A Week in the Life of High School: What it's *Really* Like Since Columbine" on its cover on October 25, 1999. Newsweek's equally positive article "What Teens Believe" graced its cover a few months later on May 8, 2000. In their more recent book *Millennials Rising*, Howe and Strauss write, "Yes, there's a revolution under way among today's kids—a good news revolution. This generation is going to rebel by behaving not worse, but better. Their life mission will not be to tear down old institutions that don't work, but to build up new ones that do." Based on their research, Howe and Strauss conclude that this generation is "less vulgar, less sexually active, less violent than the youth culture adults have created for them. This is the only teen generation in recent memory for whom this is true."

This resilient generation of kids witnessed the world explode in New York and Oklahoma City, watched the military display of "shock and awe" in Baghdad, and heard the sordid impeachment trials of a president in Washington, yet they remain optimistic, achievement oriented, and civic minded. That's nothing short of remarkable. What a great generation of kids. Though they are bombarded with violence (both real and virtual) and see more salacious stuff in middle school than we ever did, they continue to be less brutal and less sexual than the generations before them. Really, they impress me. The old goats are wrong. The "kids these days" are a terrific group of young people.

2

A Whole New World

Do you ever flip through hundreds of cable TV stations and think, "What kind of crazy world are we living in?" You are overwhelmed by a cacophony of different lifestyles, languages, and worldviews. After watching a local newscast, one of my friends told me, "I'm going to move to rural Montana to get away from the humans." Life seems so complex and unfixable at times.

Is the world really a different place than when we were kids? Perhaps all this was going on when we were younger and we just weren't aware of it. Maybe the same struggles and issues have been around for decades, even centuries, and yet youth is blissfully ignorant. After spending some time studying history, sociology, and even philosophy, I have come to the conclusion that two things are true. First, we do see the world as worse than when we were kids. In actuality, it might not be in any more disarray than it was generations ago; we just see it that way. Second, there have been significant changes in our culture over the past two generations in ways never before experienced in modern history. The world may not be much worse, but it is significantly different. To understand this well, we need a brief history lesson. Before your eyes glaze over, I can assure you that it will be brief, interesting, and relevant.

The Enlightenment was a seismic shift in history, ushering us into the era of modernity. With the Enlightenment's emphasis on intellect and ability, the world saw an explosion in the arts and sciences. A guiding notion was that through science, philosophy, religion, and art, humankind was getting better and better every day. Science could solve most of our problems, and philosophy, religion, and art could enrich our minds and souls. The Enlightenment was an extremely optimistic time. It lasted from around 1500 to about 1965, but the beginning of the demise of the Enlightenment occurred in the early twentieth century.

The two world wars and the Great Depression did much to damage the notion that the world was getting better and better and that we could solve all problems. News of tragedies was no longer spread by word of mouth, but by newspapers and radio and then television, making it increasingly hard to believe the world was getting better. In fact, many would argue that it was actually getting worse.

While these cultural shifts were occurring, some important thinkers began to challenge many modern understandings. Nietzsche said, "God is dead," and challenged the conventional notions of right and wrong. Freud said we are basically bad. Einstein stood the natural sciences on their head with his theory of relativity. James Joyce exploded modern constraints of literary structure and form with his novel *Ulysses*. Such writers as Derrida and Foucault put forth overt challenges to modernity and articulated the foundations of postmodern thought, which took hold in academic circles.

The Enlightenment took a beating, yet it survived until the 1960s. With the spurring passion of the Baby Boomers (the last great Enlightenment generation), the 1960s marked the Enlightenment's final hurrah: the Great Society, the civil rights marches, JFK, Martin Luther King. The world was going to be better again.

But then the tide turned. Kennedy and King were assassinated; the United States became embroiled in Vietnam with the Tet Offensive, the My Lai Massacre, and Kent State. Watergate broke in the early 1970s and President Nixon bowed out of the White House in disgrace.

The Enlightenment was finally dead. No one believed that human beings were basically good or that the world was getting better anymore.

Since that time, we have been living in an emerging culture that some refer to as postmodernity. More precisely, we are in a period of cultural shift from modernity to postmodernity. The themes of postmodern culture run in sharp contrast to those of modern culture's Enlightenment thinking.

Modern culture emphasized objective truth and morality; postmodern thinking focuses on personal *conviction*. Modernity celebrated the autonomous individual, whereas postmodernity puts strong emphasis on *community*. The Enlightenment was a time of great optimism, but the emerging culture is full of *cynicism*. Conviction, community, and cynicism are the hallmarks of our new culture. Let me explain with an example.

At the turn of this last century, two television shows dominated the ratings: *Who Wants to Be a Millionaire*, and *Survivor*. The first could not be more modern; the second is thoroughly postmodern. *Millionaire* succeeded on its modern themes, which were that truths are objective, propositional, and knowable. It celebrated the autonomous individual and an optimistic view of humankind. The game show rewarded factual knowledge with up to 1 million dollars in prize money. *Millionaire* is a perfect popular expression of Enlightenment thinking.

In contrast, *Survivor* is a postmodern phenomenon. Even though only one person ends up with the million dollars, the clear emphasis is on community. The inner workings and relationships within the tribes are

the hooks for the show. The decisions of the tribal council, though clearly the product of strategy, are also entirely subjective. Some individuals
are voted off because they are too competent and threatening, and others
are removed for being too weak; still others are ejected because they are
annoying or too autonomous. There is no clear standard used to judge.
The community decides what is right or wrong, favored or disfavored,
rewarded or punished.

The subtext of the Enlightenment is that we are basically good, but
Survivor makes a strong case that we are deceitful and rotten at the core.
Although it does depict some people doing noble and even heroic things,
it suggests that they are mostly selfish. The cast members say one thing to
a person's face and another when they are alone with the camera. They
consistently lie and manipulate. In the finale of the first season, Susan
rips her teammate Kelly with this speech at the final vote:

If I were to ever pass you along in life again and you were laying there, dying of
thirst, I would not give you a drink of water. I would let the vultures take you and
do whatever they want with you, with no ill regrets. I plead to the jury tonight
to think a little bit about the island that we have been on. This island is pretty
much full of only two things—snakes and rats. And in Mother Nature, we have
Richard the snake, who knowingly went after prey, and Kelly, who turned into
the rat that ran around like the rats do on this island, trying to run from the
snake. . . . I feel we owe it to the island's spirits that we have come to know to
let it be in the end the way Mother Nature intended it to be . . . for the snake to
eat the rat.

Survivor, with its cynical view of people and relationships, embodies
the postmodern ethos. As we have moved further into the twenty-first
century, *Survivor* and other reality shows have remained strong in the ratings, whereas *Millionaire* has been relegated to the leagues of syndication
with occasional primetime specials. Perhaps this stands as a cultural meta-
phor. Postmodernity ascends slowly as the Enlightenment flickers out, not
yet dead but surely dying.

WHAT THIS MEANS FOR PARENTS

The world continues to change as we move into the postmodern era.
Depending on your values and sensibilities, you may see these changes as
positive, whereas others will see them as negative developments.
Regardless, it's a new world and we would all be wise to learn how to
navigate our families through it. Today's cultural climate of *conviction,
community,* and *cynicism* has direct implications for how we parent.

Conviction

To the modern mind, truth was simple, knowable, and objective. However, as we have moved more into the postmodern era, people have begun to view truth as complex, sometimes unknowable, and deeply personal. In modern times, a position could be argued on the facts alone, but now you make the same argument and the response is typically "That's just your opinion," as if the facts were merely personal beliefs. Thus, the postmodern way of thinking is that something is true—or not true—based on whether it is *true for you*. The idea is that you have your truth and I have mine. This, of course, is a position that makes the flesh crawl for many scientists, religious scholars, and others interested in preserving notions of objective truth. To be fair, few people raised in postmodern times would doubt that certain facts are always true (a feather and a ball will drop at the same speed in a vacuum, for example), but they tend to hold the ideas that truth is subjective for *social realities*. In this sense, truth becomes a matter of one's own convictions.

It's not my intent to argue the pros and cons of this way of seeing the world. Instead, I want to accept as a given that people see social realities—relationships, personal values, societal issues—as purely matters of personal conviction. This definitely changes the way we think about parenting.

Let's take a couple of parental hot button issues to illustrate this point. Reflect on your own position regarding spanking. I don't know any parents who enjoy spanking their children, but there are people who think spanking is appropriate and others who think it is not. Is spanking okay? Can it be used sparingly as a consequence or a form of discipline? How did you come to that conclusion? Be honest: Did you review the research on it? In fact, do you really know what the research says about spanking? If I told you that children who are spanked have a 78 percent risk of being a bully at school, would that change your mind? If I told you that children who are spanked in a two-parent family have lower rates of juvenile delinquency and higher grades, would that change your mind? To be honest, I made up both those facts, but they sounded good, didn't they?

What's your opinion about day care? Have you put your children in day care? Why or why not? Studies show that day care has no adverse effects on children and can even be beneficial to some children, especially kids from poor families. Oh wait—studies also show that day care may negatively affect infants' attachment to their mothers. Actually, I didn't make that up. The research really does say both of those things. Does that affect your stance on the topic?

My guess is that your decisions about spanking and day care have more to do with whom you hang out with and respect, your general values, and your situational and economic realities than it does with what the facts really say. The postmodern mind-set is that the truth might not be fully knowable, the facts may be contradictory, and the variables are usually too complicated to base decisions purely on hard data. It is not the facts that convince us, but the disposition of our hearts.

Community

In modern culture, the individual was celebrated. The belief was that each person possessed the potential to use reason and skill to solve life's problems. Postmodern people believe that we are all flawed and selfish, so they count more on groups to problem solve and establish values.

The issue of community has direct implications for today's parents. Previous generations tended to live closer to each other; grandparents, aunts and uncles, cousins, and other family members were never far away. Today, it's pretty common for families to be scattered all over the country, staying in touch by phone, e-mail, or other technology. My brother and I live in different states, but we stay in touch a couple of times a week because we can talk to each other while we are playing an online video game. Because extended families are so scattered, nuclear families have built social supports for themselves. This isn't anything new, of course, but what is new is that these support networks are viewed synonymously with family. Pay careful attention to what you read, hear, or watch this week in the media. I bet at least once you'll hear someone referring to their community of friends and supporters as her "family."

According to social researcher George Barna, today's teens have what he calls "tribes." These are groups with fairly changeable membership, where new people can integrate into the group more readily. There is less hierarchy and more diversity than in the past. Because of this, tribes tend to do things together, and when a tribe disbands, the members often stop doing the activity. The activities can be good things, such as going to a youth group or playing paintball, or negative things such as using drugs or drag racing. Children and teens gauge their sense of right and wrong, good and bad, from their community of peers. Despite the pervasive influence of the media, they form their views of the world from their unique community.

Cynicism

Modernity was a time of great hopefulness and optimism: We really were going to make things better. However, over time many began to have doubts. Science and technology seemed to cause as many problems as they solved. Governments and corporations were exposed as corrupt. Religious leaders and institutions disappointed and even betrayed their followers. Consequently, the culture became imbued with a deep sense of cynicism, skepticism, and pessimism.

As parents we tend to see our kids through a cynical filter, even when there is evidence to the contrary. Here's a good example: When, in 1994, the Gallup organization asked American adults what percentage of crime they believed was committed by juveniles, the results indicated that they believed juveniles were responsible for 43 percent of all violent crime. The true figure is actually around 13 percent. Juveniles were thought to be responsible for 30 percent more violent crime than they actually committed.

We also tend to see the institutions that support our kids as being more suspect. We fret about our schools and school boards; we worry about pedophiles in the church; we are on guard against overzealous parents and the risk of injury in organized sports. The list goes on. We have become deeply cynical about our children and don't know whom we can trust to help us.

A FINAL EXAMPLE

I began Chapter 1 talking about a mom sitting across from me, worried about her son. I close this chapter with another mom sitting across from me, worried about her son. This time it was a fifteen-year-old boy who had become so depressed that his parents couldn't get him to take a shower or go to school. He told his father, "I don't think I deserve to live." The mom cried throughout our meeting as she told me of her son's descent into darkness.

She told me that they were desperate and would do anything to help their son. Then she added, "I really don't want him to take medication, though. I've heard about how that makes some children more suicidal."

She said this the month after the U.S. Food and Drug Administration (FDA) issued a warning about the use of antidepressants in children. I'm a psychologist, not a psychiatrist, so I don't prescribe medication, but this issue is important to me because it affects the lives of many depressed kids. As I write this, I have two articles sitting on my desk that have come out within two weeks of each other. One has the headline "Antidepressants raise risk of suicide"; the other, "Study: drugs prevent suicide." Which is it?

The studies that prompted the FDA to issue stern warnings were analyzed together, with the conclusion that drugs increased the risk of suicidal thoughts and actions by only 2 percent over a placebo. Even though some kids reported suicidal thoughts (especially when they first started taking the medication), not one committed suicide during these medication trials.

The studies involved more than 4,000 children and teens, but they had different methodologies, which made the findings less than compelling for some researchers and practitioners. For example, some of the studies did not carry out an extensive diagnostic screening on individuals before enrolling them, and others failed to exclude people who had current suicide risk, histories of suicide attempts, or family histories of bipolar illness, a disorder akin to depression, but one that often reacts negatively to antidepressants. In short, the studies were generally good and thoughtful pieces of research, but some had their shortcomings.

In 2005, a UCLA study concluded that the benefits of these medications far outweigh the risks. Dr. Julio Licinio, the author of the study, was quoted as saying, "I found that the suicide rate goes up in a straight line, year by year, from the 1960s on—right up until 1988, which is exactly the year Prozac was introduced. From there, it goes down substantially." Dr. David Fassler, a spokesman for the American Psychiatric Association, told ABC News that there is "a real concern in the medical community that the public is getting confused by contradictory media reports. As a result, people may be less likely to get treatment. That would be a real tragedy."

Early in 2005, a national news story broke in the United States about a twelve-year-old boy who murdered his sleeping grandparents with a shotgun. He had a long history of family discord, having been abandoned by his mother and passed around from one family member to another, but the defense argued that his antidepressant triggered the violence. Newspapers, Internet articles, and magazines all weighed in with experts spouting their opinions, some passionately arguing that the medicine was likely responsible, others taking the opposite view. Was the antidepressant to blame? The jury ultimately said no, but what do you believe?

This topic is relevant here because it touches on all the themes we have discussed in this chapter. The information is contradictory, so what do you believe about the use of antidepressants for children? If you had a severely depressed child, what would you do?

If you think antidepressants are to be avoided, some of your conviction may come from your perception of the companies that manufacture these drugs. Much of the debate on this topic has focused on the big drug manufacturers, some arguing that they are greed-driven machines that devour people and buy favors and approvals. Others have focused on how the

FDA, a government agency, is inept or careless. In this context, it is easy to demonize both the FDA and the drug companies.

When Merck pulled the painkiller Vioxx off the market, Raymond Gilmartin, the company's CEO, gave an impassioned testimony before Congress saying, "I believed wholeheartedly in Vioxx. In fact, my wife was taking Vioxx up until the day we withdrew it from the market." Those don't sound like the words of a man who is unconcerned about the risks of the drugs his company produces. Does that change your mind about his company's motive for aggressively pushing the drug?

This is just one of many examples of what it is like to parent in this new world. Where is the truth in all this when the facts seem so convoluted and contradictory? In a whole new world swimming with conviction, community, and cynicism, we probably base our decision on (1) how we feel about all the information, (2) what the opinions are of those close to us, and (3) what we believe about the people in charge of making or safeguarding the drugs.

You may never face the decision about whether your child should take an antidepressant, but there are countless other dilemmas you will face with your child. With so many voices in our heads, it is hard to know what to do. No wonder we have so many worried parents. The next chapter speaks to those worries and talks straight about what to do about them.

3

What, Me Worry?

I had just finished a presentation to a group of parents one afternoon when one of the moms approached me with a look of concern on her face.

"Can I talk to you for a moment?" she asked.

"Sure," I said, "What's up?"

"Well, I have a sixteen-year-old son. He makes mostly A's and B's in school. He plays soccer. He has a girlfriend and some other close friends. He gets along well with his dad and me. I don't think he drinks or does drugs. He seems to be doing well." Then she paused. "Should I be worried?"

I started to smile but I looked closely at her. She was dead serious.

Time's Jeffrey Kluger writes, "Parents have never lacked for reasons to lie awake at night. They worry endlessly about keeping their kids healthy and safe and fret about such persistent problems as teen drug use, dropout rates, pregnancy, and crime." I am constantly amazed by how much hand-wringing parents do and how much consternation they express. On the one hand, there's something good and noble about the amount of care parents show for their kids. On the other hand, the level of parental angst seems debilitating and can squeeze all the fun out of being a parent.

Why so much anguish? Perhaps it is because so many young parents didn't have good parenting models themselves. Or perhaps it is because the world is a much different place. The number one reason I hear for parental worry is that there is just too much information, too many experts and pundits, too many opinions to choose from. Parents are bombarded with so many different voices, each telling them in very authoritative tones what is best for their child. Unfortunately, most of these voices are contradictory, with one expert saying that something is good for children and the next telling them that the same thing is harmful. Consider these messages found in books, articles, TV shows, and floating around the Internet:

- Spanking is always harmful for your child. Spanking can be good for your child if done in moderation and not in anger.
- Parents must be the boss and have the final authority with children. Parents should give children a say in most family decisions.

- Teach your child the meaning of the word "no" early. Saying "no" will stifle your child's creativity and independence.
- Children need to be challenged more academically. We are pushing our children too hard in school.
- It is good to involve your kids in as many group activities as possible. Kids and families are too busy and pulled in too many directions.
- Video games are bad for children. Video games build important skills.

With so many perspectives, each backed up with a ten-year research study or some endorsement from a child-rearing authority, it's enough to make even the best parents doubt themselves. No wonder there is so much fear and so little intuition among parents today. As I speak with parents, their worries seem to fall into two broad categories: worries about the health and safety of their children and worries about the character of their children.

HEALTH AND SAFETY WORRIES

When I was a kid, the culture had a different view of children. We were allowed to roam free on Halloween night without an adult; we practically did cartwheels in the back of the station wagon with nary a seatbelt in sight; we rode our bikes at full speed with no helmet. Even then, all the same dangers were present: there were Halloween scares of razor blades in apples and poison in candy; kids were hurt and killed in car accidents at higher rates than they are now; many kids spent the evening in the emergency room with busted heads. I had my jaw shattered in a car accident and I can't count the number of times I bloodied myself on a bike, so I know whereof I speak. Today, you are a neglectful parent, almost criminal, if you let your child go trick-or-treating without being in sight or if you don't buckle him up or strap a helmet to her head. You affix floaties and a life vest to your kid, then remain hypervigilant by the poolside. You watch talk shows that spread alarm about the rise in the number of obese children, then you fret about the prospects of high cholesterol and juvenile diabetes. Instead of giving her the old sedan, you buy your teenager the car rated safest by *Consumer Reports*.

In truth, these are good developments. Children are safer and more protected than before. Our focus on child health and safety is a good thing. Parental concern is wise. But in our current culture, we are so bombarded with threat and perceived threat that it's hard to know where the true threats are. Should we be worried about violence in schools or exotic diseases or terrorist attacks or child abductors? Surely we know that more kids are hurt or killed by car and bike accidents, drownings, and house fires each year than by these other things, but it's hard to keep it all in perspective. About one hundred children are abducted each year— a very "low-probability" event—but millions of kids suffer injuries at home or in the car, which are very "high-probability" events. Regardless, parents find plenty to worry about that might affect the health and safety of their children.

CHARACTER DEVELOPMENT WORRIES

My wife, Ellen, and I were talking in the kitchen one Saturday morning when our oldest child, then only four years old, came in from the den, where she had been watching TV. She handed us a slip of paper with an 800 number written in her handwriting.

"What is this?" Ellen asked.

"It's the number you are supposed to call to get the Amazing Super Bubble Maker. It makes bubbles up to ten feet long or it can make hundreds of little bubbles. And it's only $12.99," said my junior commercial announcer.

Over the next few months, we accumulated about a half-dozen of these little scraps of paper prompting us to order some Amazing New Toy. We never made the calls, but this didn't stop our little consumer from trying to make it happen. U.S. News and World Report claims that "the average American child sees some 40,000 commercials a year" and that "the United States, with 4.5 percent of the world's population, buys 45 percent of the global toy production. American kids get an average of 70 new toys a year." No wonder Newsweek felt compelled to feature a cover story with a picture of a mom and her son going literally head to head with scowls on their faces and a headline that read "How to say 'no' to your kids: setting limits in an age of excess." Juliet Schor, author of Born to Buy: the Commercialized Child and the New Consumer Culture, says, "I found that with most of the kids I interviewed and surveyed, the more consumer culture they were involved in, the more they had conflicts and fights with their parents. Those kids who are heavily involved in consumer culture are depressed; they're anxious; they don't feel well."

Are we indulging our kids too much? Are we creating spoiled brats with a sense of entitlement? Are we raising a generation of selfish, self-centered children? These are weighty questions and the source of much concern among parents.

One Sunday afternoon, I opened up the paper and saw a full-page ad imploring parents to limit their children's TV viewing. It featured quotes from experts and statistics about the damage television inflicts on children, and it was signed by a celebrity. Indeed, several studies have come out over the past few years that draw a link between television viewing and a wide range of social ills. A 2004 study of nearly 1,800 adolescents found that teenagers who watched a lot of television with sexual content were twice as likely to have had sex as their peers who didn't watch TV with the same content. Some people have even suggested that the rise of attention-deficit hyperactivity disorder (ADHD) diagnoses is due largely to the TV-addled brains of a whole generation.

Parents also worry about the effects of video games. They say their children become deaf zombies when they pick up their game controllers. The rough content of many of the games alarms them, and they wonder whether these games might contribute to increased levels of violence and aggression in their kids. A few lawsuits have even been filed against video game companies alleging that their products caused kids to imitate the acts depicted in the games.

Are we letting our children be poisoned by TV and video games? Are we letting the media babysit our children, turning them into amoral, even violent people? These are important questions that cause reasonable parents to be concerned.

STRAIGHT TALK ABOUT PARENTAL WORRIES

If you have found yourself worried about any of these things, you can consider yourself initiated into the centuries-old fraternity of parents who have fretted about their children. It's a natural instinct to be concerned about your kids. It's good and normal. Parents who never have any worries at all about their children or about their own child-rearing practices usually aren't such great folks. They are often overly permissive or uncaring, and their children will pay the price for it in one form or another. On the other hand, parents who are consumed with worry and self-doubt cause their kids problems, as well.

What's the balanced perspective on all this? Let me suggest four guidelines to help you be a reasonable and concerned parent without making yourself crazy.

Guideline 1: Moderation in Most Things

In most areas of life, moderation is key. The same is true for worries. In truth, most kids will be just fine if they watch TV or play violent video games. Letting them watch *anything* is silly, but so is not letting them watch or play anything at all. Moderation. Kids can eat junk food and snacks in limited amounts and still be generally healthy, as long as their basic diet is balanced. Moderation. You can buy your kids new toys and let them have fun things without spoiling them if you keep it reasonable. Practice moderation and avoid the impulse to go to the extreme.

Not long ago, my oldest daughter asked for a Gameboy for her birthday. She wanted to play a series of Pokémon games that her friends had shown her. The games involved some fighting, but none of it was graphic and all of it seemed like age-appropriate fantasy play. Ellen and I felt good about this and we got her the game system. After a couple of weeks, we both noticed that she was playing it too much, so I decided to have a conversation with her about it.

"Sweetie," I said, "I've noticed you are playing your Gameboy a lot. Do you think you might be playing it a little too much?"

"Maybe," she said.

"Can you think of an idea that might help you not play it so much?"

She thought for a moment, but I knew that she is the kind of child that loves to come up with inventions and solutions, so I was pretty certain she would have a good response.

"I could make calendar of when I could play it," she said.

"Sounds great. Why don't you show it to me and mom tonight."

She scurried off to her room, found a wall calendar, and marked alternating days, giving herself one hour on each of those days. She also gave herself unlimited use on Saturdays. She presented it to us and has been following it ever since. On most Saturdays, we are in motion most of the day, doing all the kid stuff—the children's museum, the park, the movies—so it's not much of a problem, even on her day of unlimited use.

I don't feel good about kids who play video games all the time. I have one client who reports that he spends up to fifty hours a week playing online. Often he stays up until 2 or 3 a.m. when he has to get up the next morning at 6:30. That's crazy. I am concerned about kids who don't play that much but act like game addicts when they do. However, I generally feel okay about kids who play in moderation. Teaching kids this valuable skill will serve them well throughout their lives.

Guideline 2: Focus on High-Probability Issues

It is doubtful that your child will become a serial killer if he plays violent video games. It is highly improbable that your child will get West Nile virus or SARS. The odds are against her being abducted by a lunatic.

So you can keep the PlayStation, remove the breathing mask, and take the GPS locator out of their shoes.

However, there's a reasonable chance that he could get hurt in a car accident, bump his head when he falls off his bike, or drown in the pool. So buckle up, put on the helmet, and put on the floaties. Furthermore, make sure you have smoke detectors in the house, lock up your cleaning supplies if you have little ones, and keep them away from secondhand smoke. We tell our kids that the car doesn't move until everyone has a seatbelt on; we told them when they were younger that they couldn't get into the pool without life vests. These aren't unreasonable precautions; they are just wise.

We can't control everything, despite our impulse to try. The good news is that most of the nightmare scenarios—school shootings, abductions, mystery illnesses, and the like—are exceedingly rare. Unfortunately, the low-probability events often make the biggest news stories and cause parents the most worries. Use reasonable safeguards against these things, but target your concern on more likely dangers.

Guideline 3: Don't Interfere with Normal Development

For kids to develop properly, they must often do things in which there is a reasonable degree of risk. Children should ride their bikes, swim in the pool, and climb on monkey bars. Teenagers should go out with friends, get a driver's license, and play full contact sports. Don't let your worries interfere with your child's ability to do normal, age-appropriate activities. No one can promise you that there will never be an accident or a mistake, but these are normal parts of growing up. Life always involves some level of risk, so allow your children to do the things that most children of their age are allowed to do.

Guideline 4: Know Your Child

Take all that I've just said and filter it through this final point. Every child is different and presents a unique set of challenges. With that in mind, you should focus your concerns on what you know about your child. Take our video game example. If you have one twelve-year-old boy who is compliant and kind and doing well in life, then playing an action game is not going to turn him into a violent psychopath. However, if you have another twelve-year-old boy who is defiant, bullies others, and lacks empathy, then allowing him to play the same game is poison. It may not *cause* him to become violent, but it could be gasoline on the fire. The same thing is true of a whole range of worries. I wouldn't let a sixteen-year-old girl sleep over at a friend's house if I suspected they'd be drinking and having boys over, but I would probably let her do it if I felt reasonably confident that they would be going to a movie and staying up talking. I'm not naïve enough to think that parents can know all the things their kids, especially older teenagers, are doing but I know you can have a good sense of what your child is like and adjust your concerns accordingly.

FINAL THOUGHTS

We live in an emerging culture that has us off balance. We feel threat all around us. The world seems bigger and scarier than when we were children. Perhaps it is big and scary, but perhaps it always has been. When we are children, we are unaware of how much danger the world offers, but our eyes are opened as adults. We see the world with a realism and clarity that we couldn't have as children. We see danger locally and globally; we see how certain choices lead to poor results in the lives of individuals. We want to guard our kids against these bad things and help them make healthy decisions. As we parents are prone to say, we just want what is best for our kids.

The impulse to protect children is good, but it always needs to be balanced. I have met many parents who let their worries consume them. They are so full of fear that they don't enjoy being a parent. They don't have much fun—and believe me, their children notice. These parents are often so restrictive and sheltering that their kids resent them or don't get good practice at making their own decisions. They parent in fear, not in freedom. They see parenting as a minefield that they can't wait to get through without taking a misstep.

Don't let this happen to you. The world is full of bad things and life is replete with risks, but don't be paralyzed by your fears. If you find yourself parenting in fear, make a pact to start living differently. Your kids will thank you for it and you'll save money on your anxiety medicine. Live life fully and have fun with your kids.

4

Ten Traits of Good Parents

Over the past few years, I have interviewed and observed dozens of parents that I thought were especially good. I found a few common characteristics that most of them shared. This wasn't a scientific study; it was just my own systematic observation. Not all good parents have each of these traits, but they seem to have most of them. At the back of this chapter, after the following discussion of the ten traits, is an self-assessment questionnaire.

THEY HAVE A VISION FOR THEIR CHILDREN

I remember a lunch at which I was enthralled by a dad named Ken who was talking about his son named Ken. Without a hint of arrogance or presumption he spoke of what can only be called his vision for his boy. "I want him to be a man of integrity," the elder Ken said, "and someone that has the courage to do the right thing, even in tough situations." I loved what I was hearing. From that point on, I paid close attention to what parents said about their kids. I found that the better parents often spoke in these terms. They had vision for their children.

Before talking about what true vision is, let's talk about what vision is not. It is not "He will grow up to be president someday" or "He's going to be the best pro basketball player since Michael Jordan" or even "She's going to be the class president her senior year." These are things over which you have little or no control. There are too many variables outside your sphere of influence for any of these ideas to be your vision for your child. All of them are good things to hope for, but you can't have a vision for something that relies on the decisions of others.

Having a vision for your child has more to do with the character of your child, not his or her specific accomplishments. Granted, you cannot completely influence your child's character, but you can have a huge amount of input into what kind of person your child develops into. Ken may have hoped that little Ken would get good grades, go to a good college, and get a good job, but he was more concerned that the boy grow up to be a good man. This is the true nature of vision.

Many parents I know, when they found out their child was cheating on a test or bullying another child or doing some other similar concerning thing, would look at me and ask, "How could this happen? We didn't raise her to be like this." The answer comes from multiple influences. Parents cannot control the poor decisions their children make. However, it is still wise to hold a vision for your child to have certain moral qualities or character traits. Even kids who make bad choices at different times in their lives often rebound later, especially with visionary parents.

What are the character qualities that you value the most? Honesty? Integrity? Courage? Perseverance? Kindness? When you develop a vision for your child, you begin to think about how you can impart these qualities into her life. You begin to model them, discuss them, and create life experiences that develop them. The best parents I know have a vision for the character of their children and they work to make it happen.

When I ask parents what they want for their child, the number one answer these days is "I just want him to be happy." It sounds like such an obvious answer that we don't even question it any longer. What kind of heartless killjoy wouldn't want their children to be happy? Yet should this be the chief goal of parenting? I would argue that this pursuit should not be the priority for parents. The desire for happiness is understandable, but it makes better sense to desire that our children first and foremost be good. Raising people who grow up to have moral fiber and strong character is ultimately the best hope for their having healthy relationships and even healthy cultures. Vision for our children, then, cannot equal assuring their contentment and comfort. It should be helping them grow up to be people who are good.

It's worth mentioning that I have known solid parents who focused on the character of their children, yet whose kids grew up to be anything but what they had envisioned. That is certainly a possibility, but it doesn't mean that striving to be a visionary parent is fruitless. You have a much better chance of raising a person of strong character if you develop a vision for him than if you do not. The better parents talk about their kids like Ken does, wanting their children to be good rather than just to have good things happen to them.

THEY CAN BE WARM AND FIRM AT THE SAME TIME

Back in the 1960s, a professor named Diana Baumrind wrote about different parenting styles and the outcomes each produced. Over the years, others have built on her work. She talked about three parenting styles; two other researchers, E. E. Maccoby and J. A. Martin, added a fourth type. These concepts are easily understood and accessible, in spite of their academic research-based roots. Baumrind's work basically says that some parents are lax with their kids and others are firm; some parents are emotionally cold to their children and others are warm. If you intersect these two ideas, you have four quadrants, each representing a different parenting style (Figure 1).

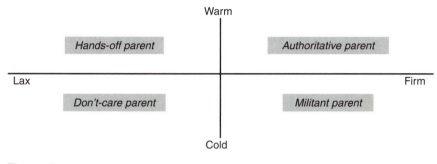

Figure 1

The worst parenting style involves no limits and no warmth. Some call this the "Don't-Care Parent" or the uninvolved parenting style. These are typically rejecting parents. They view their children like gnats buzzing around, little pests that only serve to annoy. If you want to screw up your children, you could certainly do it by adopting this uninvolved, rejecting style. You would then expect low achievement, substance abuse, and criminal behavior from your kids.

Some parents set lots of limits on their children but convey little to no warmth. This can be called the "Militant Parent" or the authoritarian parenting style. This type reminds me of Robert Duvall as the overbearing marine Bull Meechum in the movie *The Great Santini*. Meechum berated his son, Ben, as if he were one of his recruits. He screamed at Ben, humiliated him, and bounced a basketball off his head. This is authoritarian parenting in the extreme. These parents are often highly involved with their children, but they are all about the rules, expectations, and performance. They experience little emotional warmth with their children, but they reason that they are more invested in their children's character and future than in how their kids feel about them. One such parent told me, "I'm tough on him now, but he'll thank me for it later." Well, maybe or maybe not. The research suggests that this parenting style tends to produce children who are high achieving but more prone to emotional difficulties, such as depression, anger, and anxiety, in adulthood. In other words, these are often anxious kids with good grades who become depressed adults with six-figure incomes.

There is a third parenting style that involves lots of emotional warmth but little firmness and few limits. These are what I call the "Hands-off Parents." They let young children watch R-rated movies and allow teenage daughters to spend the night over at a boyfriend's house. They are also the ones who might even smoke pot with their kids. Many of these parents seem highly invested in being liked by their children or being viewed as cool parents. Others just act selfishly and don't do the hard work of parenting. The offspring of these parents often have higher rates of smoking, drinking, drug use, and sexual behavior; however, they don't seem to have the same angst as the kids raised by the drill sergeant parents.

The best style for most children seems to be the "Authoritative" style of parenting. These parents manage the sometimes tricky balance of being firm and warm at the same time. They have rules and limits as well as consequences for breaking them. They also are warmly involved with their children. The interaction with their kids is marked by lots of fun and affection. There is playfulness among the parents and kids, but there are also clear boundaries.

Research says that the children of these parents tend to have lower rates of substance abuse, promiscuity, academic problems, and emotional difficulties. My own observation is that the healthiest parent-child relationships are forged when the parents lovingly set good, respectable limits.

THEY PARENT EACH CHILD UNIQUELY

From the moment children are born, they are different from one another. Some children are cuddly; others are squirmy. Some are easy; others are fussy. Some are social and engaged; others are shy and reserved. Some have energy to burn; others do everything slowly. I know firsthand what I'm talking about. My daughters, both wonderful people, could not be more different from each other. If you picked twelve different personality variables, they would be at the opposite ends of the scales for each trait. Some parents are distressed that their children are so different, but I love it. It makes parenting a fun challenge.

I never thought I would write a parenting book, because so much of what I read on the topic advocated *systems*, *steps*, and *principles*. Frankly, I just don't think that one approach works for all children. Many of the articles and books out there promote the notion that there are some universal guidelines that can be applied effectively to all kids. I reject that idea. Children are so different from each other that it is hard to imagine a one-size-fits-all approach. So I say, "Don't parent by manual; parent each child uniquely."

From birth to college, there are countless issues that need to be approached differently for different children. Here are just a few examples:

- Toilet training
- Lying
- Poor grades
- Talking back
- Not doing chores well enough
- Being caught with marijuana

The list goes on. There are so many variables to consider—why is the child doing it, what are the relevant developmental issues, what would produce the best outcome, what are the other factors that need to be considered, etc.—that it is nearly impossible to prescribe steps that are guaranteed to work.

The best parents understand this. They don't follow some rigid system, nor do they parent each child the same way. They assess the child's unique needs and respond accordingly. They may have three children, but the same behavior from each of them may produce three different responses based on what the child needs.

I once knew a family with six children ranging in age from six to sixteen. When they ordered pizza, everyone would get two slices. Why? Because that was regarded as "fair." If one child got more than another, there would be lots of bickering and whining. To be fair, everyone got the same amount. Now do you consider this to be fair? I don't. In a family, fair doesn't mean equal. Fair means that everyone gets what he or she needs. A six-year-old can have one pizza slice and a sixteen-year-old can have five slices and it can still be fair. Fair does not mean that everyone has the same bedtime, the same privileges, or the same responsibilities. The sixteen-year-old should have a later bedtime, more privileges, and greater responsibility than his youngest sister. The best parents don't focus on fairness defined as equality. Instead, they focus on ensuring that every child gets what she needs.

Let's take a frequent source of conflict between parents and their children: bad grades. Two of your kids come home with D's on their report cards. Should you ground them, take away TV, lecture them, or not mention it at all? Some combination of the above? None of the above? The true, but perhaps unsatisfactory, answer is that it depends. There are lots of factors to consider, including the age of the child, whether there was good faith effort put into the class, and whether the child has some learning or attention issues. I think it makes good sense to restrict TV or video games for a period of time with a middle schooler who isn't doing his homework. At the same time, I would completely support the parent who takes the position with a high school junior that there are natural consequences for poor grades (e.g., reduced chances of admission to her college of choice) and leave it at that. But you might ask, what about the teenager who isn't motivated to go to college? How do you motivate her? The answer is that you may not be able to, and it is certainly doubtful that grounding her for the next grading period will change her internal motivation all that much.

Good parents know they have to use good judgment in order to respond uniquely to unique children. They don't follow rigid or depersonalized steps. They give all of their children what they need and they do it in individualized ways.

THEY TRUST THEIR INSTINCTS

Soon after my first child was born, I was reading a parenting book as part of my research and I was shocked to see it strongly advocate that parents should *not* trust their instincts. The premise of the book was that your instincts are so flawed and erring that you must follow carefully laid-out steps in raising your child. To be honest, I couldn't agree less. Parenting cannot be reduced to a cookbook. It would be nice if you added the right ingredients in just the right amount and eighteen years later, the perfectly cooked human popped out. It is a flat-out lie that there are steps and principles that apply in every circumstance and that, if followed zealously, will produce a guaranteed result.

Individuals are too complex and too unique to be parented by unwavering steps and principles. The best parents I know realize this. They know that there are some principles, such as the need for consistency and warmth, but they trust their instincts. This makes them flexible and helps ensure that their approach fits well with what their child needs.

Recently, I was leading a support group for parents of difficult kids. On one particular night, the topic was creative discipline. After the group, one of the moms said to me, "I can't do what you are saying because you've got all this specialized training and degrees. I can't think of ideas like you do." The belief that there is some sort of secret knowledge that is possessed by only certain people is a major barrier for many parents. I don't minimize the importance of certain professionals, but when parents stop trusting their own good instincts and start relying too heavily on experts, then something important is lost.

The best parents I know have good instincts and they trust them. There are lots of curveballs and sticky situations that come your way as a parent for which no formula is sufficient. You have to be able to trust your gut.

THEY THINK WIN-WIN

In his brilliant book *The Seven Habits of Highly Effective People*, Stephen Covey says that the individuals who do best in life tend to interact with others so that everyone wins. They don't think about how they can prevail over the other person. Instead, they consider how everyone can get what they want. There is no doubt that I have seen this in action with the best parents. Even with their hot-headed children and surly teenagers, these parents think about how everyone can win.

I'm fond of saying that good families are not democracies, but they are benevolent monarchies. The parents must be in charge. However, this does not mean that the parent must always "win" and the child must not. It is possible much of the time for everyone to win and for the parents to maintain their authority.

Sometimes the key to thinking win-win is *The Art Of The Reframe*. When you reframe something, you set it in a different light so it looks different, more manageable, clearer. This is a skill that not everyone has, but it is an invaluable one to learn. Here's a tough situation that could use a reframe: Suppose your seventeen-year-old daughter wants to stay out until 1 a.m. with friends, including kids that you know to be heavy drinkers. They'll be going from house to house and there's no telling where they'll end up. With a firm voice and steely gaze, you tell her she can't do it and begin to generate options with her, such as having friends over and going out with another, more responsible girl. She is furious! She says you try to control her all the time. Other parents let their kids stay out until 1 a.m., she informs you, and next year in college she'll be able to go out whenever she wants. It ends in a lot of screaming and histrionics. What to do?

I usually say that if two people both want the same thing, they can usually get it. For example, if a couple wants to follow a budget for the year in order to have a better vacation, they can make it happen. But in this example, it appears that parents and daughter are at cross-purposes. The daughter wants to go out with partying friends; the parents don't want her to go. How can this impasse be resolved? That's where the art of the reframe comes in. Let's rewind this and start again.

The truth is that the girl and her parents don't want different things. At root, they actually want the same thing. The parents want her to be safe; the teenager ultimately desires this (though she may not be as tuned in to the dangers as her parents are). The girl wants to be more independent and to make her own decisions; the mom and dad want her to be a responsible young adult. Reframing takes the focus off the superficial issue—whether she can go out with these friends until late—and moves it to the deeper issues, namely safety, responsibility, and autonomy. The discussion then shifts to negotiating how everyone can get what they want. The parents are right in insisting on assurances of safety. The daughter is right that she needs practice making her own decisions before college. Somewhere in this discussion, I bet they can work out an agreement where everyone wins. Idealistic, you say? Not at all. I do this every week in my office with some of the most rigid, cantankerous kids (and parents) that you can imagine.

Some conflicts cannot be negotiated out. Those times are inevitable in child rearing. That's when you must simply be the boss and hold firm. However, the best parents try to minimize locking horns with their children. They model flexibility, good problem solving, and collaboration. They think win-win.

THEY CO-PARENT WELL

Imagine this situation: Grayson is fifteen years old and he is going on a cruise with his parents and younger sister, Ally, an eleven-year-old. Because his parents want him to have a good time, they allow Grayson to invite his friend Carl, another fifteen-year-old from his class. The disagreements between the parents start the first night. Mom thinks the boys should stay with them during the port excursions; Dad thinks they are big enough to look out for themselves. Mom is concerned that the boys are sneaking alcohol; Dad lets them sample margaritas at dinner. Mom wants them back in their room by midnight; Dad argues they can set their own curfew. Mom worries they are hanging around two older girls too much of the time; Dad lets them stay unsupervised in the girls' room. Finally, when Mom blasts Dad for his lack of limits, he calls the boys aside and says, "Grayson's mother wants you to be back by midnight tonight and tomorrow you need to stay with us." When the boys object, he says, "I know. She just worries about you."

You might find yourself agreeing more with the perspective of one parent than the other in this story, but there is a lot at stake here. It is not just about whether fifteen-year-olds should be allowed to stay out all night on a cruise ship. It's about the message that these parents are sending to the children. When I consult with parents, I typically feel free to express my opinions about how I might come down on certain decisions with different kids, but I stress the importance of taking a position together. Oftentimes that means negotiating privately then presenting a unified front, each backing the other up. I am talking about a big concept called *parental alignment*. It's good for kids, and the best parents do it all the time.

Research shows that kids do better in two-parent families. Much resiliency research has found that single-parent homes are risk factors for children. Single moms I know certainly recognize they are at a huge disadvantage from the get-go. Don't get me wrong: kids raised by their mom without a dad certainly can turn out to be brilliant entrepreneurs, athletes, musicians, or ministers. That's the whole point of this book: teaching parents how to use strengths to outweigh weaknesses, no matter what their situation. It's just oftentimes more effective to have two parents instead of one.

On the contrary, if you have two parents who are on two totally different pages, you don't have much advantage at all. After a presentation on parenting styles, I had a dad come up to me and ask, "What if I'm the authoritarian parent who lays down the law and she is the hands-off parent who is warm and nurturing? Is that a problem?" My response: "It's a problem." He went on to argue that they each give their kids half of the best parenting approach, the "warm and firm" style, just in two different bodies. I told him that it would be best if it lived in the same body! Equally important, I said, was the need to parent consistently with each other as a team.

Many years ago, I had a conversation with a pastor whose wife had left him and taken their four children. He said that their differences over child rearing had led to the split. When I pursued this further, he told me that he felt that kids needed limits and boundaries and his wife never set them. He said he was always making rules and giving consequences and she was always undermining him and not enforcing the punishments. As you know, every story has at least two sides, so when I spoke with his wife a few months later, she told me that he was harsh and unreasonable and she felt the need to shelter her kids from him. I'm sure the truth was somewhere in there, but it struck me how important it is for the adults to be together in parenting.

The best parents I know parent well together. They confer, they agree, they give and take. They speak with one voice to their children. They don't argue in front of their kids about discipline or consequences. More important, they never directly or indirectly undermine the other in front of the children. I have met many parents who tell their kids with a wink that they know Dad is a little too strict or Mom tends to overreact and this sort of thing. That's usually bad news. I actually love it in my therapy sessions when I have kids or teenagers show exasperation about how their parents *always have to agree with each other*. How horrible! Many kids will experience the negative effects of dissension and division between their parents, but few will ultimately lament their parents presenting a united front.

THEY KEEP SHORT ACCOUNTS

A while back I had a mother in my office going on a tirade about her son. As the crowning proof that he was a defiant and disobedient boy, she told me how he had pierced his ear after she forbade him to do so. When I spoke with the boy about this, he acknowledged that it was true, but he added—almost as an afterthought—that this was over a year ago. The more I got to know this family, the more I realized how angry this mom was at her son and how deeply her grudges ran. She kept a record of wrongs that was a mile long. Two years ago, he broke her figurine by throwing the ball in the living room. Three years ago, he left the fence open and the dog escaped. Four years ago, he pushed his baby brother down and the little boy had to get stitches. And the list went on. There was no question that he was a difficult child, but she was a deeply resentful woman who reviewed his transgressions constantly.

What I have found among good parents is the opposite of this woman's need to hold onto her child's past sins. The better parents keep short accounts with their kids. They let past failures and misbehaviors go. They don't hold on to their children's mistakes indefinitely. Although they give appropriate consequences for wrong behaviors, these parents know how to start fresh every day.

Since I work with a lot of difficult children, I have noticed that this is one quality that seems particularly evident in really good parents of tough kids. These moms and dads make real efforts to start off each day anew. With some kids, especially ones with behavior problems, this is extremely tough. A child's tendency to repeat the same behavior is especially hard to forgive. But the better parents know how to let go and move on.

I'm not suggesting forgetting or excusing every misbehavior. If your child lies to you repeatedly, it doesn't mean that you have to trust her every day as if it never happened. If your teenager is caught with beer in his car, for example, it doesn't mean you don't take the keys for a while or, as a client's mom recently said, "until he is thirty." Keeping short accounts does not mean that you can't have long-term consequences. Instead, it means letting go of the anger and resentment that often linger well after the misbehavior. When a child errs, you should establish a con-sequence, but do it in an almost businesslike manner. Release the bitter-ness over what happened. This is what it means to keep short accounts.

THEY ENJOY THEIR KIDS

When I speak to groups, I frequently say that the best parents enjoy their children. One night after I spoke, one of the moms raised her hand and gently asked me whether I was laying a guilt trip on parents who had difficult children. She said that some children are simply hard to like. I agreed with her basic point, but I held my ground. You really can make a choice to enjoy your children, even if they are tough. You may at times want to twist their heads off, but you should always be able to grit your teeth and focus on one enjoyable thing about them.

There are two camps of people who struggle to enjoy their children. The first are the parents who just don't like their children. The kid is too different from them or too similar to them, or they have nothing in com-mon, or whatever wild reason. What do I tell these parents? Choose to move toward your child anyway. Choose to do some things that he wants to do. Find a way to enjoy him.

The other camp houses the overanxious parents. They are so worried all the time that they don't stop to recognize what a cool person their kid is becoming. Not long ago, I had a mom sit across from me and give me a litany of all her worries: my son doesn't study enough, he speeds in his car, he hangs around kids I think are bad, he stays up too late, he doesn't eat well, he fights with his brother, and the list kept going. I simply told her that she was so worried about these things that she wasn't taking time to enjoy him. He was a great kid. His grades were good. He had a great sense of humor. He made mostly good decisions for himself. I told her that I didn't want her to look back on his childhood and feel regret that she never stopped worrying enough to enjoy him.

I am encouraged by the parents who persist with their kids, even when it is tough to hang in there. Some of them have to make a conscious deci-sion to move toward their children and keep desiring a relationship with them when it would be so easy to shut down and get cold. My hat's off to you! You're doing really hard work.

THEY HAVE FAMILY TRADITIONS AND RITUALS

Before we got married, my wise and witty mother-in-law, Mannon ("like cannon with an 'm,' " she explains), told Ellen that if we eloped rather than going through a big wedding ceremony, she would "give us a thousand dollars and hold the ladder." Despite her appeal, we didn't take her up on the offer and planned a big wedding instead.

There is a part of your engagement when you are doing all this wedding planning and you find yourself about two clicks away from a nervous breakdown. This was certainly true for me and Ellen. In the middle of the craziness and stress, though, we had one particularly fun date where we cooked dinner and just enjoyed being together. It was like a calm shelter in a furious storm. The table was lit by tall pink candles, and so the evening became known as our "pink candle night." When we talk about pink candle moments now, we know we mean a time when things are going well despite stressful events around us. We have had many of these moments in our marriage and we always connect them to something concrete that helps us remember the event. This practice of choosing visual reminders of significant events has become a ritual for us.

My colleague Dr. Frank Gaskill did some of his early research on the importance of family rituals in the lives of children. He found that rituals and routines protect families against stress and the effects of trauma. This is true even in families where there are significant problems. For example, adult children of alcoholics had consistently more positive life outcomes if rituals, such as dinnertime or bedtime routines, were observed consistently by the nonalcoholic parent. Aggressive teenage males also got their behavior on track if positive family rituals were reported during their early childhood. These are just a couple of examples of the benefits of family rituals, even in tough family situations.

Dr. Gaskill said that it isn't the ritual itself that is so important, but what meaning the child attaches to the ritual. For example, identical twins, raised in the same home, were asked to describe a family ritual that they recalled from their childhood. Both agreed their mother's giving them a cookie after school each day was a consistent ritual. The twins were interviewed separately and when asked about the meaning of this, one twin fondly recalled, "That cookie told me my mom loved me and thought of me during the day." The second twin stated, "I hated that cookie . . . it was a daily reminder of how poor we were . . . only one cookie." Dr. Gaskill said, "While the rituals are important, the ritual itself is not the protective mechanism. The actual protective factor is the meaning behind the ritual as perceived by the child."

When I think about my family now, I am grateful that we have lots of traditions and rituals, both big and little, frequent and infrequent. Ellen makes dinner for all of us and we eat as a family. We talk about the "highlights" and "lowlights" of the day as we eat. I read to my girls nearly every night before I put them to bed. We both take each girl out on "dates" and do something special for each one, which usually involves some sort of purchase! We have family game nights on Fridays. We vacation with the same five families every year. We spend Thanksgiving with Ellen's parents in the mountains and Christmas with my parents at the beach.

One night after I finished reading to Abbey, I said that her new pajamas looked cute. She reminded me that they were a Christmas present. She added, "Every year we open our pajamas the night before Christmas." She's right. On Christmas Eve, the girls open two presents and the first one is always new pajamas so they will look especially cute in the pictures the next day. I mention this story not to brag about our family tradition, but to say that Abbey has noticed this custom and she remembers it. I bet that she'll remember the pajama tradition into her adulthood.

Rituals and traditions ground children with the feeling of security and stability. They give a family shared experiences that help children remember important aspects of their upbringing. They help children feel cherished and important. The best parents realize this and are intentional about adding these important customs to the lives of their children.

THEY DON'T PARENT FOR AN AUDIENCE

A few years back, one of my teenaged clients came in one afternoon with bright electric blue hair. I saw him in the waiting room and laughed out loud. It actually looked pretty cool, but it was so blue I had to bite my tongue to keep from singing the Smurf theme song. When we were in my office, I asked how people were responding to his new look. He said the kids at school mostly liked it, the guys on his basketball team gave it mixed reviews, but the older folks at his church just stared at him. I asked him how his mom felt about taking him to church in front of all the disapproving people and he said, "She doesn't care what they think." He shrugged as if to say it was no big deal to either of them. "Good for her," I said. I felt proud of his mom. Let me add that this kid was a great guy. He was one of my favorite clients and he had a great, open relationship with his parents. I'm glad they didn't care whether he had blue hair. I actually kind of liked it.

The best parents I know don't make choices based on avoiding the disapproving looks or behind-the-back comments of others. Instead, they do what is best for the child. For my blue-haired boy, the best choice was to let him be an individual and do his thing.

When our family was in the process of moving, some friends were kind enough to let us stay at their house as we transitioned to our new home.

Their house was gorgeous. It was in one of the best neighborhoods in the city and sat right on a fantastic golf course. We noticed that the neighborhood directory listed the names of everyone in the development as well as the work titles of each resident (the words "president," "owner," and "chief executive officer" were not uncommon). It also listed the schools each of their children attended. Let's just say that there weren't a lot of public schools listed. I'm sure the neighborhood association would deny it, but the message of the directory was clear: you will be judged by your title and by the school your child attends. I wondered how subtly these parents felt pressure to "keep up with the Joneses."

I once tested a boy who was in an elite private school. He had a learning disability in reading and some major attention problems. It was clear that he would not do well in this school. I advised his parents to consider a particularly good public school in their area that had a reputation for excellent resource services. The parents balked at the idea. When I pressed them on this, they said that they just wanted to see if it could work where he was because "he's got his friends there and the teachers know him." What they didn't say—but what was the obvious subtext of the conversation—was that no child of theirs would go to a public school and be labeled with a learning disability.

In some circles, private school is the only choice; in others, if you don't homeschool your child you are practically engaging in child abuse; still others extol the benefits of church or parochial school as the only way to go. I have recommended all three, depending on the needs of the child. And that's my point. Decisions such as this one should be driven by what each child needs and not by some social pressure that the parents feel. Depending on the unique needs of the child, any of these can be the absolute best decision.

My point is that the best parents don't necessarily care whether their child has a conventional haircut or drives a car that shows the family's buying power. Instead, they tend to resist being socially pressured to make their children or themselves appear good. In other words, they don't parent for an audience. They don't regard their child as an extension or reflection of themselves. They make judgments about what is best for each kid and then they go for it, regardless of what their friends or neighbors or parishioners might think. Even if that means blue hair.

ASSESSMENT OF THE TOP TEN TRAITS

Color in the circle that represents your best answer. Add up the numbers inside the colored circles (either 1, 2, or 3) to come up with a total score.

	Not true	Somewhat true	Very True
1. I have a vision for the character of my child	①	②	③
2. I am both warm and firm in my parenting style	①	②	③
3. I parent each of my children differently based on what they need	①	②	③
4. I have good parenting instincts and I follow them	①	②	③
5. I tend to think "win-win" in conflict situations with my children	①	②	③
6. I collaborate and parent well with my spouse	①	②	③
7. I don't hold a grudge with my kids when they do something wrong	①	②	③
8. I enjoy being with my children most of the time	①	②	③
9. I have established traditions and rituals for my family	①	③	③
10. I don't make parenting decisions based on what other people will think	①	②	③
Total score			

There are no norms for this quiz, but here's a good rule of thumb for scoring:

26–30 = Excellent!
22–25 = Good
18–21 = Fair
 0–17 = Needs work

Three Practical Questions

1. Which of these traits are your strengths?
2. Which of them need the most work?
3. How are you going to work on them?

5

Kids with a Hope and a Future

For the winter program, the overheated cafeteria of my daughters' school has been transformed into a theater, where my wife and I sit shoehorned with the rest of the parents waiting for the show to begin. After we have endured the Madonna song "Holiday" screeching over the speakers no fewer than four times, two kids finally take the stage. They are the anchorman and woman, guiding us through the holiday celebrations of different countries. The curtain opens to reveal a chorus of kids all grinning and nervous, singing songs about the season. I scan the faces of these young people, all different colors—white, black, brown—and think about their futures. Who would be a good spouse and parent? Who would grow up to be a scientist, an artist, or a doctor? Who would break his mother's heart? Who would treat her loved ones badly? It's an occupational hazard, I guess, to fill such light moments with analysis, but I do it more as a parent than as a psychologist. I often look at my own daughters and wonder what life will be like for them. We can guide them and give them all our best parenting and loving, but we can't control their outcomes. There is a ghost in the machine.

This uncertainty leads some parents to overmanage their kids, as if somehow they can hold back every negative influence. Unfortunately, keeping the bad guys out is a nice notion that just doesn't work. Kids can still find pornography on the Internet, buy pot at the best private schools, or get their homeschooled girlfriends pregnant. Even the best of kids can make bad choices or have bad things happen to them. That is the nature of the world.

Some parents go to the other extreme and throw up their hands. They don't even try to make wise choices for their kids. They bring their six-year-olds into R-rated movies or tell their sixteen-year-olds it's okay to drink, as long as they do it in the house with their friends and don't drive. It's mind-numbing foolishness, yet they always have some rationale for why it's helpful or at least why it won't hurt.

For most of us, it's hard to find the right balance of restrictions and permissions. Even if we did, we know there are so many other factors that will ultimately determine the outcomes of our children. We want what is best for our children and we'll cling to anything that gives us answers.

We read articles with such titles as "Seven steps to raising a successful child," but these formulas start to ring false after a while, especially as our kids get older and life gets more complicated.

As my father used to say, "What's a mother to do?"

THE REAL DEAL

During the lifetime of this Millennial generation, a solid body of research has emerged that has identified not only the risk factors associated with kids' problems, but also the protective factors that were found in individuals and families who do well, even in the face of adversity. This research has allowed us to answer questions as never before. More important, these studies point us to new ways of helping children, their families, and even entire communities.

We've known for years that there are certain risk factors that tip the scale in favor of trouble. They may be traits that the child possesses, such as a difficult temperament or chronic medical problems, or they may be experiences outside of the child, such as abuse, neglect, or family chaos. Each of these risk factors, in essence, moves the child one step closer to trouble.

However, over the past decade and a half, we have identified an almost equal number of protective factors that tip the scale in the opposite direction, in favor of good outcomes. Some of these protective factors are internal to the child, such as intelligence and sense of humor. Others are part of the child's world, such as consistent discipline and having a mentor. Each of these protective factors tips the scale one notch closer to a hopeful future.

When I first heard about resiliency theory, I was intrigued, but I disagreed with one fundamental assumption. The research claimed that the various risk and protective factors were essentially equal in strength. In other words, the factors were not weighted. Major risk factors such as poor attachment and abuse were lumped in with such seemingly minor risk factors as multiple moves and siblings born within two years of each other. Likewise, big-time protective factors such as good problem-solving skills and positive goals for the future were mixed in with innocuous items such as extracurricular involvement and having alternative caregivers available to the parents.

At the time, I was the clinical director of a large agency that served really wild and aggressive kids. This seemed like a perfect group to use with this model, so we developed a checklist of all the known risk and protective factors. I had my team of clinicians assign weights to each of the factors on both sides, and we used their average rating for each item. Using that checklist, we rated about a hundred of these teenagers using both the weighted scale and an unweighted scale, then we tracked them over the course of a year or more, measuring them again with behavior ratings. What we found was that the weighted checklist was no better at predicting their functioning than the unweighted checklist. It wasn't the weight of the various factors; it was the *sum* of the factors that made the difference. The resiliency research, much to my surprise, was right. These findings have led to this simple equation:

Sum of protective factors − Sum of risk factors = Prediction of outcome.

We just take all the known protective factors and add them up, then subtract the total number of risk factors. If the number is positive, you are likely to have a positive long-term outcome. If the number is negative, there is likely to be trouble ahead. And it appears that the strength of the number equals the strength of the prediction. In other words, a score of 15 is much more likely to yield a long-term positive outcome for a child than a score of 5. Similarly, a score of −10 probably means more heartache down the road than a score of −2.

There is no guarantee in any of this, of course. The ball could take a funny hop at any point. A teenager with tons of protective factors may still get into a car accident, make a life-altering bad decision, or just fail to move forward. Other teenagers with far more risk factors end up turning their lives around and becoming successful. However, for the most part, my own experience lines up with the research: the greater the number of protective factors, the greater the chance of a good future.

A FABLE AND SOME FACTS

There is an old fable that has been told for years of the frog and the scorpion. The frog sat by the river's edge, minding his own business, when a scorpion approached him. The frog eyed him suspiciously.

"Give me a ride across the river on your back," said the scorpion.

"No!" said the frog emphatically, "You'll sting me and I'll drown."

"Why would I sting you?" asked the scorpion. "If I did that, we'd both drown."

The frog thought about this for a moment and then, impressed by the logic, agreed to give the scorpion a ride. The scorpion climbed on the frog's back and they set out across the river. When they were in the middle, the scorpion's tale twitched nervously. Then he violently stung the frog in his back.

"Why'd you do that?" yelled the frog. "Now we'll both die."

"I couldn't help it," said the scorpion, "it's my nature."

The point of the fable is that people are true to their nature even if it kills them. Therapists see it all the time. People find it easier to kill their marriages, kill their brain cells, or kill their integrity than to change core aspects of themselves. Sometimes it is impossible to remove bad things from the essence of a person. On the other hand, it is much easier to add good things in.

Although we struggle across our lifetimes with bad habits and maladaptive patterns of relating, we may find it easier to take on new skills and change our life circumstances in ways that help us. These good things that we add into our life—what we have already termed protective factors—help move us toward health, despite the adversity we face or the bad habits we have created. Maston wrote, "Studies of resilience suggest that nature has provided powerful protective mechanisms for human development." Resiliency theory is built around the notion that what is right with us is more powerful than what is wrong with us.

By adding protective factors into our lives, we increase the chances of good outcomes in a wide range of areas. Research has uncovered protective factors associated with such things as increased cancer survival rates, favorable response to psychological and medical treatment, prevention of youth aggression and violence, decreased risk of suicidality, high academic achievement, lower rates of substance abuse, decreased vulnerability to depression, and rapid rebound from traumatic events.

HOW GREAT A NEED EXISTS?

The Search Institute surveyed nearly 100,000 children in sixth through twelfth grade in 213 towns and cities across the United States. Their intent was to determine what percentage of children and adolescents experienced various protective factors, which they called *developmental assets*. Their research led them to conclude there were forty of these developmental assets—both internal and external—that improved the outcomes for children. Their research also found that less than half of the students surveyed had twenty-five of the forty. In other words, most kids did not have a majority of the protective factors. There is clearly no shortage of opportunity to increase protective factors in the lives of children and adolescents.

According to the Search Institute's survey, the least present developmental assets were involvement in creative activities (19 percent), living in a community that values youth (20 percent), having a caring school environment (24 percent), being given useful roles in the community (24 percent), and reading for pleasure (24 percent). The assets that were most present in the lives of the young were having a positive view of personal future (70 percent), family support (64 percent), involvement in a religious community (64 percent), and school engagement (64 percent).

Other research found that a low overall number of protective factors also adversely affected families. For example, some studies show that many marriages don't survive because the risk factors of the family outweigh the protective factors. Also, families who struggle long after a traumatic event often have relatively few protective factors to bolster them.

There is little question that a great need exists. If we understand protective factors, then we can build them into our children, teenagers, and families. This leads us to a new approach in parenting.

A NEW APPROACH

Focusing on protective factors presents an extremely practical model for helping our children and our families. It is a new way of thinking for many parents. For those who have been misled into believing that there are seven simple steps to raising healthy (or emotionally intelligent, respectful, or highly motivated, etc.) children, the notion of adding protective factors seems to resonate more honestly. This approach to parenting has two simple parts:

1. Consider the Whole Child

Old approaches emphasized how to correct specifically what was wrong; the focus was often narrow and limited. The approach is far broader here. It not only focuses on all aspects of the person—the mental, emotional, behavioral, physical, and spiritual—but also emphasizes the larger context of each individual. A person's relationship with significant others and communities, such as school and peer groups, is vitally important and is seen as an opportunity for increasing health.

2. Focus on Strengths

Rather than pointing out weaknesses, this approach looks to strengths—what is going well already and which positive things are missing but can be added into a person's life. The fundamental belief is that increasing strengths is both powerful and practical. This is a great opportunity for parents to build upon the individual strong points they see in each of their children.

BUT DOES IT WORK?

One of my favorite parts of my job lately has been the chance to work with extraordinary kids who want to do extraordinary things with their lives. Most of my career has been helping people shake loose of pathology, which is the bad stuff. However, I've seen an increasing number of clients, mostly adolescents, who come in at their own initiative looking to go from good to great. These are kids who want to become more competitive with college admission or improve their sports performance or more fully develop a business idea.

We work on building their existing strengths, then identifying any gaps. It is a fun, energizing, and encouraging process. Just this week, a client told me he had just shot a round of seventy in golf (which is a good score), another told me he had been accepted into a competitive music program, and still another shared his business plan for a new startup. I've got a great job and I'm enjoying it more than ever because of these invigorating kids.

I also have used this resiliency model in working with special needs kids. It's commonplace to find parents of special needs kids who want the one thing—the magic bullet—that will help their kid. It could be a drug, a specialized therapy, a nutrient shake, an innovative summer camp, or a new technology. These quests for the Holy Therapeutic Grail rarely end well, if they end at all. They go on and on from one promising thing to the next. Bolstered by the testimonies of others who claim tremendous success with the new diet or vision therapy or gifted clinician or whatever, the belief persists that there is something out there that will set everything right. Yet, despite their deep longing and earnest searching, I'm sorry to say that there is no one thing that will cure all ills or ensure good outcomes.

This is why this new approach not only makes good sense, but also gives hope. Instead of one thing that will fix it all, there are many things that will increase the chances of a brighter future for each child. Certainly, the magic bullet theory has its appeal, but it rings hollow and false. How many books have been sold, lectures attended, or products purchased that offer one powerful answer to a complex problem? To be sure, some of these have merit, but they tend to overpromise and underdeliver.

This parenting model is built on the resiliency theory that strengths can be built into the lives of any child, regardless of risk factors, and tip the scale in favor of good things down the road. To parents of special needs kids, I say, Don't abandon therapy or other helpful interventions, but reframe your thoughts about the meaning and importance of those interventions. Each might equal one protective factor added to many others and not be the one magical cure. Keep doing what works, but take a broader view of how to help your child.

Whether your child has special needs, is a budding genius, or is somewhere in between, the resiliency model makes good sense. It is straightforward. It's free of the usual psychobabble and hype. Most important, it is practical and easy to get your head around. It is full of things you can do to give your child a better hope and future.

In the coming chapters, I will elaborate on this model by giving detailed descriptions of protective factors that you can add into your child's life, regardless of age, gender, or life circumstance. Some of the model focuses on individuals and families, whereas other aspects focus on building healthy communities.

The first thing I need to do is dispense with the negative side of the scale. The risk factors usually can't be changed, and yet they must be acknowledged. They are either experiences that have already happened or traits that are hardwired into the child. My colleagues and I have conducted extensive research with hundreds of children and families, and in the next section I will present the risk factors we found. I won't linger on the negative, but you should know what you are up against.

6

Risk Factors

As a psychologist working with a county agency, I saw kids who had more strikes against them than you can imagine. Some lived in violent, drug-ridden neighborhoods, some were mentally handicapped, others had been to court numerous times or had mothers who abused drugs while they were pregnant. I really enjoyed these kids, even though I sometimes felt they didn't have a chance. They were feisty and strong; many of them found ways to survive, despite the odds. When they didn't do well, it was always frustrating and sad. Daily, I saw the impact of risk factors on their lives. These risk factors were not just some abstract, academic notion. They were real things that hurt real people and shredded many futures.

As a psychologist working in private practice, I tend to see healthier, more intact families. Despite this, these kids still have risk factors, ranging from a shy child who has been sexually abused by a neighbor to a delinquent teenager who skips school by day and fights with his parents by night, filling his downtime with large amounts of alcohol and marijuana. No matter where you are, the world is full of risk and trouble. It's unavoidable.

Before most researchers ever thought about developmental assets or protective factors, they examined the impact of risk factors on children. We've known for decades that negative experiences, traits, or conditions can adversely affect individuals during their formative years. As I've said above, you can't do much about the majority of these risk factors. They are either things that have already occurred or they are conditions that you cannot change.

Nearly every child has some risk factors, so the point here is not to alarm you but rather to educate you about issues that tend to cause young people trouble in their lives. These factors fall into five categories. I will list the risk factors, then discuss some aspect of each category in a section titled "Bringing It Home." I am not going to elaborate on each of the risks, but I want you to be aware of all of them.

❏   Relational Risk Factors

- Has lots of problems with people in authority
- Has severe conflict with more than one family member
- Has at least one sibling who has gotten into serious trouble
- Has problems forming attachments and bonds with others
- Hangs around with friends who get into trouble

Bringing It Home

Healthy relationships are a sign of a healthy person. The opposite is true, too. Unhealthy relationships are a sign of an unhealthy person. Individuals with poor relationships tend to have a whole range of negative outcomes in their lives. They are often poor spouses and parents; they don't get along well with bosses and co-workers; they get into more trouble. These problems are usually evident from childhood, so a huge relationship risk factor for a kid involves predominantly unhealthy relationships.

❏   Physical Risk Factors

- Has chronic or major medical problems
- Was exposed to toxins in the womb
- Has an IQ in the mentally handicapped range
- Was mostly shy or withdrawn as a young child
- Is hyperactive and impulsive

Bringing It Home

Whereas some risk factors are the product of the child's environment or experience, physical risk factors are prewired. They just *are* and can never fully go away. The unfortunate result for these risk factors is that they have a domino-like effect on areas of life beyond the physical. These kids have a harder time socially, which leads to a tendency to feel bad internally, in turn creating emotional instability that may affect their school experience. They are incredibly vulnerable.

When I wrote my dissertation, I had to test many hyperactive kids for my study. Ah, I remember them well. One had the phone cord wrapped around him within minutes of starting the test. Another had his hand in the fish tank. Several others were upside down on the couch—or under it! It was a sight to behold. Since then, I've had more hyperactive and impulsive clients than I can remember. Many of them have done well in life and some have made it through college. But for those who have been successful, it was never easy. They had to fight to overcome their disability, and there were many days of discouragement and thoughts of throwing in the towel.

Attention-deficit hyperactivity disorder—known as ADHD in our culture—is a condition that causes people either to have trouble keeping their attention focused or to be hyperactive and do things without thinking about them first, which is referred to as impulsivity. Good research indicates that between 3 and 7 percent of all children have ADHD, and that most of those folks were born with it. You tend to see it passed genetically; it's not a discipline or parenting problem that causes true ADHD. Simply stated, it is a wiring problem.

Early in my training, I worked in a pediatric clinic one day a week. Kids would come into the clinic and we would do all the testing, interviewing, data collecting, and observing necessary to make a decision about whether a child had ADHD. I remember standing behind a two-way mirror watching a little hyperactive boy play in the next room. I asked the psychiatrist beside me, "Why would you give a hyperactive child a stimulant? That doesn't make sense to me. How does it help them?" Her response? "We don't know."

At that time, doctors didn't know why medicines such as Ritalin helped these bouncy kids; they just knew that stimulants usually helped hyper children settle down. Years later, we know the answer. Kids with ADHD seem to have at least one area of the brain—usually in the frontal lobe—that is actually underactive, as if it's asleep. This part of the brain governs such things as planning, concentration, and controlling impulses. When a stimulant hits it, it "lights up" with more electricity and blood flow, so it works more efficiently. In brain scans, children and teens with ADHD have less activity in this areas than their peers. In fact, if you were to scan the brain of a twelve-year-old boy with ADHD and the brains of nine other twelve-year-old boys, a specialist could pick the ADHD child out of the group based on their scans alone. There would be little "craters" of inactivity in the ADHD child's brain compared with the other boys. Knowing this, it now makes sense that giving a hyperactive child a stimulant can cause that sluggish part of the frontal lobe to "wake up" and help him concentrate and stop to think before he acts.

Children and teens who are hyperactive and impulsive are at a risk for many negative outcomes, including poor school performance, a greater risk of car accidents when driving, greater social rejection, higher rates of substance abuse, and a greater chance of having some other psychiatric condition such as anxiety or depression. It also makes them more likely than other children to be aggressive or even violent. Later in life, they have a harder time holding down jobs and maintaining relationships than their peers. In short, it stinks. The romantic notions that ADHD people have advantages because they are more creative, have more energy, and can multitask better are mostly myths. It is a condition that tends to negatively affect the outcome of the lives of many people.

❏ Behavioral Risk Factors

- Has a history of alcohol or drug abuse
- Has a history of delinquent behavior
- Has been involved with the court system
- Has skipped school more than once
- Is failing school or has dropped out of school
- Does many risky or dangerous things

Bringing It Home

Some psychologists talk about the three aspects of a person that need to be addressed in therapy: thoughts, feelings, and actions. When children enter treatment, it is most commonly because they are having some trouble with the third aspect, their actions or their behavior. Certain behavioral risk factors are inherently problematic, such as engaging in delinquent behavior, skipping school, or abusing drugs. However, some behaviors are risky because they are barometers for attitudes that cause other kinds of trouble for a child down the road.

There are many kids with serious drinking and drug abuse problems who are living right under your roof. The most common drugs of choice are still alcohol and marijuana. Most kids don't ever mess with the harder drugs. I've certainly had my fair share of clients who have gotten desperately messed up on cocaine, ecstasy, and even heroin. However, the majority of kids who use drugs tend to drink alcohol or smoke pot. Some use both, but it is curious to see how kids will use only one and not the other. A few of my private school kids think that only drug addicts smoke pot, yet they go to parties every weekend and get falling-down drunk. The kids who only smoke marijuana do it because "everyone they know" does it; they often report not enjoying alcohol much at all.

Many of the pot-smoking kids are almost militant in their defense of their drug: it is natural, they say. It helps you relax and enjoy things better. It has medical benefits. No one has ever died of smoking pot. It's way safer than alcohol—and that's even legal. And so on. I wish I had a nickel for every time I've heard these arguments in my office. Marijuana may be "safer" than alcohol in some respects, but that is like saying the flu is safer than the West Nile virus.

It usually doesn't help much to try to convince these kids that their beloved substance is potentially harmful to them. These kids have gone through drug education classes and they know to "Just Say No." A couple of times my pot-smoking clients have imitated the counselor on *South Park* and said in a nasally voice, "Drugs are bad, mmm-kay?!" In light of this, my approach is rather to work on their ability to make good decisions and to increase their motivation to change. This motivational approach tends to be effective, though it usually takes some time.

Although I make a point of not being just another lecturing grown-up, I can tell you that smoking marijuana remains a risk factor for kids. In some respects, their arguments are right. People who smoke pot are less likely to be violent than those who drink alcohol, for instance. However, marijuana has negative effects in more subtle ways. The biggest problem seems to be that marijuana significantly decreases a person's motivation. It does it in such an understated way that people are often unaware. They know they don't care and they just don't care that they don't care. Not surprisingly, their school achievement, work performance, and level of follow-through on responsibilities are lower than those of people who don't use the drug.

Alcohol is clearly dangerous. It has a tendency to disinhibit people, making them much more likely to do things they would not do if they hadn't been drinking. People under the influence of alcohol are more apt to get into fights, break the law, have random sex, or say things they wouldn't normally say. Adults who drink wine for dinner or have a few beers while watching a football game are often able to regulate how much they drink and make wise choices. When teenagers drink, it is typically in a group with other peers without adult supervision. The mixture of alcohol, a large group of drunk kids, and all the pressures that go with adolescence is often a wicked combination.

The signs that a teenager may be developing a problem with drugs or alcohol include, but are not limited to, such things as

- Unexplained declines in grades
- Negative changes in attitude and mood
- Extreme defensiveness about drug use or drinking

- Evidence of spending much time thinking about drugs (conversations, e-mails, Internet searches, drawings, jewelry, T-shirts, etc.)
- Paraphernalia
- Frequently having red eyes or carrying eye drops
- Prescription medicines being used faster than they should be
- More secrecy than before about actions or possessions
- Hanging around with peers suspected of substance abuse
- Getting into serious trouble (with the law, at school, etc.) because of use
- Continuing to use even after being caught
- Using when alone

I'm surprised by how some parents regard the drug use of their kids. They often say, "It's a phase and she'll get over it" or "I did it in high school and I turned out just fine" or something like that. It may be true that experimenting with drugs is fairly normative in teenagers. However, it's also true that, as a parent, you have a job to do that involves not making it easy for your child to continue using drugs or drinking. The parents who have the ability to keep the lines of communication open while setting good limits and boundaries tend to do best. The parents who are preachy, overly harsh, or overly reactive tend to do almost as badly as the ones who are too permissive in this area. Not all experimentation will lead to addiction, so you don't need to explode if you become aware of your child's drug use or drinking. At the same time, you don't need to endorse it or support it either. The key here is *balance*. Take it seriously but don't freak out. Set the limits but don't go crazy with the restrictions and consequences. If your child has a definite problem, get it assessed and then take the necessary steps.

Recently I had an initial meeting with the parents of a boy who seemed depressed and had declining grades. I asked whether there was any chance he could be using drugs. "Oh, no! If he was, we could tell," they assured me. When I met with the boy, he told me confidentially that yes, he had been smoking pot every day for the past year. I've had lots of similar experiences. Once I had a boy who wrote up a fake biology project with timelines and due dates and convinced his mother to buy him hydroponic equipment so he could raise plants in the attic. She, of course, never checked to see what exactly was growing in the attic. She would have been shocked to find lots of little pot plants basking in the glow of the lights she had purchased. Some parents need to be a little more skeptical. Don't constantly interrogate but be aware of the possibility that your beloved son or daughter may be up to more than you know.

❏   Belief Risk Factors

- Has an overly high or overly low opinion of self
- Expresses many negative attitudes
- Thinks violence is a good way to solve problems

Bringing It Home

There are certain attitudes or beliefs whose mere existence poses some risk for the kids who hold them. Why? Because these attitudes translate to real-life problems in both behavior and relationships.

I heard a speaker say that the problem with kids today is not that they think too poorly of themselves, but they think too highly of themselves. He went on to make the argument that our culture of narcissism is more harmful than having people with low self-esteem. The truth is that he is half right. The research has found that it is not good to have an overly high opinion of oneself nor an overly low opinion of oneself. Either extreme is unhealthy and out of balance.

I had a client, a teenage boy, who was extremely narcissistic but couldn't see it. Even after we talked about this in the most direct terms, he said that he was not even close to being like that. He was so convinced that when I proposed the idea of mailing out checklists (using modified wording from the diagnostic criteria for Narcissistic Personality Disorder) to the people who knew him best, he was all for it. We worked on the wording of each item together until he felt that each one was fair and clear. We had items on there such as "Seems to feel he is entitled to special treatment from others" and "Doesn't seem to care about the feelings of others." Then he gave me a list of twenty people who knew him well—friends, family members, teachers, coaches, and so on—and gave me permission to mail them out with a letter of explanation. I got a 100 percent return rate, which I took to be a good thing. Before I revealed the results to him, I asked him what he would consider to be a problem. He said, if any item on the checklist was rated by a majority of the people. He told me that he didn't think any of them would be rated that high. I showed him the tally sheet. All but one of the items were rated by a majority of the people. Having already agreed that this constituted a problem, we then set to work.

On the other side of the scale are those who have an overly low opinion of themselves. People with miserable self-esteem don't do as well in school or in their jobs and in their relationships. One of my clients was a boy in the midst of a major depression. He said that there was nothing good about himself. He was ugly, stupid, uninteresting, and a little bit mean. He agreed with me to do a personal inventory where we took an honest look at his strengths and weaknesses. A curious thing happened in that exercise. When he looked at himself honestly, he had more good qualities than bad. And the good qualities were pretty cool things: social skills, good sense of humor, musical ability, and insight. The exercise forced him to reevaluate his self-image. If we hadn't challenged his overly negative perspective, then he would have been at risk for many future problems.

Once I met a tough, streetwise boy, one of those kids with thick necks and meaty arms who look like they could tear you limb from limb without breaking a sweat. His name was Teck and he was one scary-looking dude. He had just pummeled another boy in a locked residential unit because the other kid had said something about having relations with Teck's sister (whom the other boy had never met, incidentally).

Teck was in an isolation room and had had enough time to cool down when he agreed to talk with me. We discussed what had led up to the altercation and I simply asked, "What else could you have done?"

The guy looked at me like I was insane. "What do you mean?" he asked.

"If you had to do it over again, what could you have done differently?"

"Nothing," he said plainly. "That's all you can do."

I've met my fair share of Tecks in my day, especially in residential programs. Surprising, though, is the number of kids, usually boys, who are in regular schools, part of regular families, living in regular neighborhoods, who hold similar views. Some kids have deeply held beliefs that violence is the best—and perhaps only—way to solve problems. Someone insults your momma? Hit him. Someone takes your seat on the bus? Fight him. Someone bumps you too hard on the playground? Knock him down.

It's obvious that this is not exactly the way to win friends and influence people. These kids end up in a world of trouble, mostly because they continue to do violence despite the consequences. These are the children who get kicked off the bus, cut from the soccer team, and suspended from school, but if someone messes with them, they are ready to rumble.

❑ Experiential Risk Factors

- Has been a victim of discrimination
- Has never lived in one place for very long
- Lives in an area with a lot of crime
- Has had a serious physical injury
- Has experienced serious trauma

Bringing It Home

Some children have risk factors in their lives just based on where they live or how long they've lived there. A 2001 study of more than 900 children and their parents in four rural North Carolina counties found that multiple moves was one of the five greatest risk factors that affected the mental health of the children in the study, right up there with lack of parental warmth and a family history of mental illness. These experiential risk factors often have tremendous effects on young people.

I see kids for a variety of reasons in therapy, but trauma issues have become my specialty. The irony is that I am the most squeamish guy I know. After you read the following story, you will have some insight as to why.

Have you noticed how you remember all the little details of the best days and worst days of your life? I was nine years old. My little brother, Brian, and I were at Wayne Money's house that afternoon. *Match Game* with Gene Rayburn was on television. Wayne's little brother, Aaron, thought the mashed potatoes were "dirty" because they had pepper on them. I remember all these little things.

My aunt Charlean picked us up later, taking Brian and me to her house to play with her train set and chase her cats around. I got wheezy from the cats, my asthma kicking in. So the three of us hopped into Charlean's Volkswagen Beetle and took off for home. In those days, VW Bugs had the engine in the rear and nothing in the front. The body of the car was so thin that you could usually see the road through parts of the floorboard.

Brian roamed untethered in the back seat. He stood in the footwell directly behind Charlean, hitting the back of the driver's seat with an ice scraper. She reached behind to push him back up onto the seat, her eyes leaving the road.

Exploding glass.

Blackness.

More than thirty years and I still remember it like it was last week.

Someone grabbed me under the arms and dragged me from the passenger seat. Here's what I saw: a telephone pole in the middle of the car, windshield shattered, blood on the dashboard, and teeth.

"Those are my teeth," I thought to myself.

I was right.

Some man laid me gingerly on the pavement. It was a heavily traveled street, so people came running within seconds of the wreck. One guy in a Navy outfit saw me, and a look of horror twisted his face. Another woman burst into tears.

Charlean was running around in hysteria, crying and darting back and forth from one side of the car to the other.

I remember thinking that something really bad had happened to me even though I didn't hurt very much. I had a headache, but nothing else seemed to be too painful. I knew I had blood on me. I knew I could only mumble when they asked me questions. But I wasn't in excruciating pain.

Brian was nowhere in sight, but I judged by Charlean's frantic rush from one side of the car to the other that he must be on the other side, probably laid out on the street like I was. The ambulance finally came and after many minutes they carried me into it. That was when I saw Brian. His head was cut wide open and looked bloody and purplish. He drifted in and out of consciousness; paramedics kept calling his name to keep him awake.

My parents got to the hospital quickly. They were calm and reassuring (although I found out later that my father got sick to his stomach after he saw us). Brian got stitched up. Charlean got stitched up and calmed down. I went in for surgery. My jaw was shattered. All my lower front teeth were knocked out. I had multiple facial cuts.

We got cool presents from all our friends while we were in the hospital. I remember that the stuff was all stashed under my bed, making me feel good about having it there. I was doing fine until they let me walk down the hall and look at myself in the bathroom mirror.

I was certainly no stranger to injuries: dog bite on my chin, sliced finger from a broken Coke bottle, multiple wrecks on the bike, falling off the fence onto my head on the concrete driveway (and knocking all the hair out of the top of my head, giving me a monk haircut for a few weeks), full wheelbarrow tipping over and cutting my knee open, and I won't bore you with the rest. None of these injuries prepared me for what I saw.

I looked into the mirror and saw a huge stitched-up gash on my chin and a more grotesque one between my nose and upper lip. Other little cuts and bruises covered the rest of my face. I got depressed almost instantly. Seeing my reflection was the worst part of the whole ordeal.

Weeks later, after we left the hospital, Brian told me he kind of liked his scar. He said it made him look like Frankenstein, which he thought was cool. My mother said he looked nothing like a monster but Brian would not be dissuaded.

When the time came for Brian to get the stitches out, we all went together to the surgeon's office. The nurse called his name.

"Brian?"

"Raaaarrrrrh!" he said.

"Ooooh!" said the nurse in mock fear.

"My mother says I look like Frankenstein," he offered.

The nurse cut my mother a look that I'll never forget, a look that said, "You evil woman!"

Some weeks later, we were having tomato soup for lunch. Some of it dribbled down my chin. My mother said it looked like I had a hole in my chin. I wiped my chin with a napkin and some more soup dribbled out. Not down, *out*. I *did* have a hole in my chin! The soup had made its way down the wires that went through my gums and had come out the stitches' holes.

A year and two plastic surgeries later, I was playing baseball. First baseman. Booms of thunder in the distance. It started to rain. A few drops sprinkled on me, and I was overwhelmed by a strange feeling. Things suddenly looked distorted. My heart raced. Something bad was happening. I bit my lip and kept on playing. No one realized what happened. Weeks passed and it hit me again in the bathtub. I was splashing around and the feeling hit again. This time I panicked. I jumped out of the tub and yelled for my mom. I couldn't describe to her what was happening.

A few more of these "spells" and my parents took me in for an EEG. They thought I was having seizures. I got rigged up with about fifty electrode thingies glued to my head. The results were fine though. Nobody could figure out what these spells were, so nothing was done. They continued to hit me out of the blue for the next year or so until I found a way to make them stop. I would look down at one spot, take deep breaths, and talk myself through it. After a while, they went away and I didn't think of them too much again.

Skip ahead ten years. Now I was in college, sitting in a class called Abnormal Psychology. An amazingly odd guy, well-known on campus for moaning and wailing loudly in his dorm room during the night and making bizarre comments in class, walked in late. He talked loudly and with a heavy speech impediment.

"Is this Abnormal?" he shouted as he swung the door open.

"You better believe it," said the girl beside me.

I started laughing, putting my head down on the desk to muffle my snorts. I loved this class. As the semester progressed, we talked about various abnormal conditions and diagnoses. One day, we talked about panic attacks. Sudden uncontrollable episodes of panic that seize a person. Heart races. Chest tightens. Think you're going crazy.

In a flash it came to me.

"So that's what those were," I thought to myself. A full decade later and it all made sense. I quickly figured out the triggers, as well:

Thunder = sound of car crashing.
Rain or splashing in the tub = sensation of blood on my face.

All entirely unconscious but completely real. This was the beginning of my fascination with psychology. I share this story to let you know a little bit about myself, but also to make the point that traumatic experiences can affect our relationships, our self-confidence, and our emotional functioning. For me, the experience ultimately made me stronger, more confident, and more empathetic than before. But it was at a pretty great price.

* * *

Nearly every child has some risk factors. I certainly did growing up. My own children do now. Despite this, take courage! Protective factors can save the day.

Introduction to Protective Factors

One afternoon, after I'd finished presenting on protective factors to a group of mental health professionals, a clinical social worker came up to me and said something that has stuck with me. She said, "I came here because I wanted to use this information in my work, but I'm leaving here thinking about my own kids and I'm feeling hopeful."

In a cynical world, hope is often in short supply. Too often, people feel let down by things in which they had put their hope. A great feature of the resiliency model is that it doesn't make outlandish claims, boastful promises, or seem based on dubious evidence. It is just a well-grounded idea that has an elegant simplicity. It doesn't require expert consultation to make it work; it is accessible to everyone. And it has some solid evidence to back it up. In that sense, it is hopeful.

Since many of the risk factors are fixed or unchangeable, most of the previous chapter focused merely on describing the risks that children face. However, in this section, I not only want you to understand the protective factors, but also hope to equip you with good tools that will allow you to develop them in your own children. Our research found twenty-one protective factors that are associated with good outcomes for children. They seem to cluster into six broad categories, with three or four factors in each one. The exciting thing about these factors is that the majority of them can be enhanced in some way. In fact, only two of the twenty-one—early temperament and high intelligence—are locked in. With the rest, the door is open. When you are done reading about these protective factors, my guess is that you will feel encouraged, empowered, and, most important, hopeful.

7

Emotional Protective Factors

Somerville is a small, densely packed industrial town that sits in the divide between the lower Charles and the Mystic River, just outside of Boston. In some areas, the city is packed with urban professionals and college students who live near Harvard and Tufts. One of the neighborhoods there, Davis Square, was named one of the "hippest places to live in the United States" by a trendy magazine. Working-class families populate the east side of the city. This town also has its fair share of poor families and people scraping by on welfare, with nearly one out of every seven of its children and elderly living below the poverty line.

More than forty years ago, a team of researchers decided to track 500 boys who grew up in this city to see how well they did in life. About a third of them had IQs that were below average; two-thirds of them lived in poverty. Over the four decades, researchers watched these boys move into adulthood.

What they found was very interesting. The subjects' intellectual ability didn't seem to have much bearing at all on how well they did in their jobs or how well they did in life. The outcomes of their lives correlated more with how well they understood and handled their emotions. The boys who controlled their anger and tolerated frustration did well. The boys who got along better with other people did well. Conversely, the ones who had poor social skills and more conflict with others did poorly. The ability to understand and manage emotions held the key to a happy and healthy life.

I've known many kids who had great potential but whose lack of skill in dealing with emotions kept them stuck. One such guy was a seventeen-year-old named Ben. His parents thought he was depressed because he was not motivated to do well in school; he seemed sullen and withdrawn. It sure seemed like he was depressed. But as I got to know Ben, I realized that he wasn't depressed at all. He was just emotionally void. He had a condition called Asperger Syndrome that made it extremely difficult for him to understand emotions and to connect with other people.

Ben had one of the highest IQ scores that I had ever seen. He was in the 99.9th percentile of intellectual ability, which means if you took 1,000 seventeen-year-olds at random and ordered them by IQ, he'd be first in line. Despite this, he was failing several classes and had low grades in a couple of others. He didn't see the point of it all; he simply didn't care.

Ben was also a cool-looking guy. He had long brown hair, piercing blue eyes, and high cheekbones that made him look like a Calvin Klein model. In fact, he'd been approached twice in the mall by people who wanted him to do modeling for their agency. Despite this gift, he didn't have any close friends and none of the girls at school were interested in him, mainly because he couldn't carry on a conversation. He wasn't a self-absorbed narcissist; he was just not interested in people.

Ben remained undiagnosed throughout his childhood because he was smart, good-looking, and talented in music and math. However, I first began to suspect he had Asperger's when his mother said, "He can tell me every detail of a book that he has read, but if I ask him a question about a character's motivation, he just looks at me blankly and says, 'What do you mean?' "

Despite his strengths, Ben seemed ill equipped to make his way through life. Although he is an extreme example, his case underscores the emotional component required for being successful in life. He didn't do well in school not because he didn't understand the material, but because he didn't care and didn't have a passion for it. He had no close social relationships not because he wasn't attractive to others or lacked talent, but because he didn't understand others or care much about them.

Lots of smart people have been hobbled by their lack of emotional intelligence. One study gave a group of graduate students a series of intelligence tests, personality tests, and structured interviews. The researchers tracked them for several decades after they got their Ph.D.s and asked experts to review their resumes and rate how successful they had been in their career. They found that emotional skills were four times more important than cognitive intelligence in determining professional success.

In our own study of several hundred children, we found three emotional skills that served as protective factors for kids. The first is the ability to talk about feelings openly and honestly. The second is the ability to care about the feelings of others. The third is the ability to feel bad after doing something wrong. Some kids are naturally skilled in these areas. In other children, these skills can be developed.

❑ Talks about Feelings Openly and Honestly

Daniel Goleman is a Harvard-trained psychologist who was a science writer for *The New York Times*. His specialty was writing about new research on brain functioning and human behavior. When his book

Emotional Intelligence hit the bestseller list, it created ripples in fields as diverse as the financial industry and preschool education. The concepts were so resonate in the business field that it spawned its own cottage industry with books and videos and lecture series. Professionals who work with children also realized the importance of the concepts and they, too, developed materials to help educators and mental health professionals.

P. Salovey and J. D. Mayer, two researchers, were the first to use the term "emotional intelligence," but Goleman's book put it into the mainstream. Emotional intelligence refers to a wide range of qualities, such as self-awareness, impulse control, empathy, and social deftness that allow a person to manage her self and her social relationships well. Emotional intelligence has these components:

- *Identifying emotions*—being able to tell when you are having a feeling and being able to distinguish one feeling from another
- *Managing emotions*—being able to control feelings so they don't get out of control or get the best of you
- *Using emotions*—being able to take emotional energy and channel it into things that are healthy and constructive

The first component of emotional intelligence, identifying emotions, is essentially synonymous with the first emotional protective factor, being able to talk about feelings openly and honestly. This is the foundation for the remainder of emotional intelligence. Children must learn what they are feeling before they can control those feelings or use them constructively.

You can do a few things to help your children talk about feelings. The first is to make sure they can tell the difference between feelings. This may sound obvious, but for some kids, it takes practice. Ask your child to think of a time when she felt happy, sad, mad, and then scared. After each emotion, ask her what thoughts were running through her head when she had the feeling. Then ask where she felt it in her body. Some people feel certain emotions in their stomach, others in their chest or head or even arms. See whether the feelings are different from each other. If all the feelings are felt in the gut, then ask, "Where else do you feel 'mad' in your body?" You want to help her become aware of the cognitive and physiological cues that come with certain feelings. Pay careful attention when she describes times she has strong feelings. She might say she felt sad when she really is describing a time she was angry. Educate her about the difference between feelings when that happens. Help her practice identifying feelings and talking about them.

Some children are extremely emotionally expressive. They find it easy to say whether they are frustrated or scared or sad. Others always keep their parents guessing, which can lead to a kid's unhealthy understanding of emotions. There are at least three emotionally unhealthy styles for kids. Here's a description of each, as well as some thoughts about what you can do—and in some cases, not do—to help your child.

1. Feeling Forgetters

These kids take all their feelings and stuff them way down, trying not to think about them or examine them too much. When they are frustrated, they just stuff it. When they are sad, they try to forget about it. When they are anxious, they pretend nothing is bothering them.

Unfortunately, trying to forget or stuff feelings typically comes with a price. I liken it to a pressure cooker. As the steam builds up, it must have a release valve. For most healthy people, the pressure is vented by using either written or spoken language. Words give form to feelings and allow them to be more readily understood and processed. That's why just talking about something often makes us feel better. If the valve is blocked, then the pressure must be released some other way. For kids, it may come out in the most indirect ways—headaches, stomachaches, panic attacks, unusual fears, and other assorted reactions. If the "forgotten feelings" aren't expressed, then prepare for a blowup. That's when these kids have big meltdowns—either intense anger outbursts or uncontrolled sobbing.

Feeling Forgetters believe that feelings are bad and must be avoided at all costs. Perhaps they saw this modeled for them in their home. Maybe they had some particularly unpleasant experiences with emotions in the past. Either way, it's a pattern that is hard to break.

You can help children who bury their feelings by having regularly scheduled times when they can talk about their emotions. Facilitate this by asking such questions as "What was the happiest part of your day?" and "What was the most frustrating part of your day?" We often ask our girls over the dinner table, "What were the highlight and lowlight of your day?" After they answer, we ask them to tell us the emotion connected to those events. "Did you feel sad or mad when that happened?"

Encourage older kids to keep a journal to write down their feelings. Many of my teenage clients keep online journals, sometimes with Internet postings for all to see. Believe it or not, I think this is a generally good practice. One word of caution for parents, though: people talk and write differently in these online journals than they do in other parts of their life. The talk is much more aggressive and profane. The content is more shocking. Perhaps it is because it is more anonymous (even though they are being revealing). Perhaps it is because they are writing during times when they are most emotionally charged up. My guess is that it is a little of both these things, but also because it is adopting a persona. It is a developmental process when kids "try on" a new aspect of identity. It's sort of like saying, "Here's the version of me that cusses a lot, talks about drugs and partying, and is into really edgy stuff."

Some of my kids have allowed me to read their online journals; some have even requested that I do. At first, I thought that they were being dishonest with me in our sessions. The kid was telling me that he wasn't using drugs, but was bragging online about getting high, for example. I've come to see that, oftentimes, the online version is entirely fictional. More than one kid has told me that the online self is more like a role-playing game. I say all this to make a simple point: if your child has an online journal, *do not read it*. It may give you wrong information that will make you crazy.

If you have a Feeling Forgetter, then the antidote is to get him talking. If he can't talk it out, then encourage him to write it out. Explain the importance of using language to process feelings and give him plenty of opportunities to do it. For these kids, this requires persistence. They don't do this naturally, so it takes a lot of patience, encouragement, and practice.

2. Affective Airheads

Unlike the kids we just discussed, the affective airheads don't try to avoid or ignore feelings. Instead, they simply don't have a clue. They don't know what they are feeling, what triggers certain feelings, or how to distinguish one feeling from another.

The most common expression that I have seen is usually boys who mistake every negative emotion for anger. If something frightens them, they get mad. If they experience something that would make other people sad, they get mad. If they feel lonely, they get mad. They simply cannot distinguish one feeling from another.

The other version of this is the child who cannot tell you how she was feeling during any significant emotional event. You ask her how she felt at her grandmother's funeral and she says, "I don't know." You ask her how it felt to have the bully threaten her at the bus stop and she says, "I'm not sure." With these kids, you get the sense not that they are trying to avoid a known feeling but that they really have no clue about their emotional world.

For Affective Airheads, you want to help them distinguish one feeling from another. Feelings have at least three components: the affective part, the cognitive part, and the physical part. When you are angry, you emotionally feel mad, you have mad thoughts, and it hits you in your body in a specific place and in a unique way. Anger should be experienced differently than fear, happiness, sadness, or any other emotion.

If you have a younger kid like this, try the following exercise: Place a big sheet of butcher paper or poster board on the floor and have him lay down on it on his back. With a washable marker, trace the outline of his body. Then give him the choice of several colored markers. Ask him to pick out a color that looks like happy, then mad, then sad, then worried, then any other feeling you want him to identify. Have him close his eyes and think of a time when he felt really happy. When he opens his eyes, have him tell you about it. If it rings true, then ask him to close his eyes again and tell you where he feels it in his body when he has that happy feeling. After he opens his eyes, have him draw that feeling with the "happy" color on his body tracing. Repeat this for each feeling. Discuss it and process it as you go. For older kids, you can try something similar, but use a body outline on a regular sheet of paper and skip the actual body tracing.

You have to teach Affective Airheads this level of emotional attentiveness in step-by-step fashion. They need help in identifying feelings, telling the difference between feelings, and knowing how to respond to each feeling in a healthy way. Like any skill, developing this requires lots of work. Be patient.

3. Emotional Extremists

You've seen these kids before. Perhaps you even have one in your own house. When they are happy, they are overjoyed. When they are sad, they are sobbing and despondent. When they are angry, it is a nuclear explosion. Now, there's nothing wrong with living life passionately and fully. The problem comes when these kids have no ability to regulate or modulate their feelings. Their emotions simply overtake them, causing them—and those around them—much trouble.

Younger children are nearly always Emotional Extremists. They simply lack the developmental capacities to control themselves when they feel something. You know when a toddler or preschooler is mad or sad, that's for sure. However, as children mature, they should develop more self-control. They should rule their emotions and not the other way around. Some kids, though, never seem to get the memo. They are so emotionally intense that it begins to affect many parts of their lives, especially their relationships.

You can teach Emotional Extremists skills to control their feelings. Remember: the goal is not to stop having the feelings; it is to help them manage the feelings as they occur. This process takes time and practice, but it is still one of my favorite things to do in therapy. You can do some of the work at home even before consulting a professional. Begin by explaining the bigger goal: control feelings, not eliminate them. I say this because if a child believes he is trying to "stop feeling so angry," then he will usually give up quickly because it doesn't work. I help him identify things that make him mad (or anxious or sad or whatever the target feeling). We come up with a list of at least five to ten things and talk about which ones are the biggest triggers. From there, we talk about the things that start to happen when he gets mad, such as clenching his fists, raising his voice, or breaking things. I have included my checklist below.

Extreme Emotion Early Warning Signals

❑ Break things	❑ Have thoughts of hurting someone	❑ Say mean things
❑ Clench my fists	❑ Hit someone	❑ Start breathing fast
❑ Clench my jaw	❑ Hit something hard	❑ Stomp on the floor
❑ Cry	❑ Hit something soft	❑ Tear up things
❑ Feel upset in my stomach	❑ Kick something	❑ Throw things
❑ Fight someone	❑ Refuse to do things	❑ Use bad language
❑ Get a headache	❑ Run out of the room	❑ Yell

I take all the checked items of things he does when he gets mad and put them in order from the first things that happen to the last things that happen. We then pick one or two of the early warning signals, things that happen most of the time near the beginning of the anger pattern. Those one or two things become the signals that alert him to the fact that he is starting to get mad and he must use his strategies.

The strategies for controlling feelings can often be relatively simple things, such as taking deep breaths, counting backward, or taking a self time-out. I explain that anger (or any other target emotion) is a feeling and that to control a feeling you must do something with your mind and your body. I have children pick one "mind" strategy, which is usually something that serves as a distracter, such as backward counting. My favorite of these, by the way, is the word jumble, where I ask kids to find one word somewhere in the room and make other words with it. For example, if I see the word "brother" in my office, I can form the words "the," "broth," "her," "hot," and many others out of it. It diverts my attention away from the source of my anger for just enough time to gain control of myself.

I also have kids pick one "body" strategy that involves doing something physical. I don't tend to get a lot of good feedback about the three deep breaths, though this is the one that gets pushed a lot by parents and clinicians. I do, however, hear kids tell me that it helps if they are able to do something athletic or physically intense, such as push-ups, jumping-jacks, running, shooting baskets, and so on.

There is a fair amount of debate about the whole notion of doing something semiaggressive when you are mad, such as hitting a punching bag or walloping a pillow. I have met many kids who feel quite relieved by hitting something that doesn't hurt them or get broken. Sometimes this becomes a successful strategy and helps them control their anger well. One boy is allowed to go outside and hit a dead tree with a baseball bat. The tree is dead and the bat is sturdy, so no one's getting hurt. I have another client who goes outside and digs in the garden when he is mad. I have several who work out or hit a punching bag in the garage when they are boiling. In each case, it is helpful to them, and their parents report that their overall anger control is better. Most of these kids tell me that they just need to "push off against something" or words like that. They don't necessarily need to be destructive or hurtful, but they feel so physically tense that they need to discharge it somehow. It's a judgment call, but for some people, this seems to be a good way to express their feelings.

I use the example of anger because that is often the most intense and distressing emotion that kids express, but the same process applies to sad feelings, anxious feelings, or any other feelings that are getting the best of a child. When I work with a kid on emotional control, I explain that it is like any skill that requires rehearsal and practice. You aren't going to be good at it the first time or the second or third time, but eventually you will develop skills. This is true whether the issue is shooting free throws, working on a skateboard move, learning a musical instrument, or gaining better control over your feelings.

One final thought to help kids talk openly and honestly about their feelings is to make sure that *your* style promotes emotional expressiveness. Some parents clearly communicate that it is not okay to express strong feelings. Here are four parenting styles that do not produce emotionally healthy children.

1. Trivializing Style

I remember sitting in my office one day with a father and his middle school son. The kid was clearly depressed. He moped around in a perpetual frown, rarely leaving his room or doing anything other than going to school. There was also a long family history of depression, including two suicides within the past decade. The boy sat across from the dad, staring at the floor as his father spoke.

"I don't get it," said the man, "It's not like we don't do things for him. He's got a ton of games. He's got his own TV. We pay for him to go to private school. We even bought him a cell phone this summer. He barely does anything around the house. He's just lazy if you ask me. There's nothing to be depressed about."

You mean except for having a father who's an insensitive jerk?

Trivializing parents tend to minimize or dismiss their children's feelings. They tell them that it's stupid to be scared of something or that boys are sissies when they cry. The consistent message to the child is that their feelings don't matter or are ridiculous. Children who are raised by these parents tend to feel ashamed of their feelings later in life and often have a hard time expressing them openly.

2. Hostile Style

During one of our usual shopping sprees to Wal-Mart not long ago, I was standing behind a family in the checkout line. The children, a brother and sister, were acting silly but they weren't being too disruptive. The girl had something in her hand and giggled as her younger brother tried to pry it away. The mother wheeled around at them and screamed, "SHUT UP! Both of you, shut up!" Not "stop it" or "calm down" or even "be quiet," but "SHUT UP!" I was jolted by the response because it was so out of proportion to what prompted it. Sure enough, the kids shut up.

Hostile-style parents tend to get angry at their children for expressing any intense emotion. If a child expresses anger, it is met with anger. If she shows fear, it, too, receives an angry response. Nearly any strong feeling produces an angry, hostile response from the parent. Consequently, these children learn that it is not safe to express feelings openly, so their emotional expressions tend to wither over time.

3. Uninvolved Style

At the park, I watched a dad with his five- or six-year-old son. The dad sat on a bench not too far from me and read the paper. His son was digging in the sand and flipped some up into his eye. As expected, he ran back to his father, furiously rubbing his eye and crying.

"What happened?" the dad asked.

"I got sand in my eye," said the boy.

"Well quit rubbing it," said the dad, returning to his paper.

"I can't!" said the boy, "It hurts."

"It's just sand," said the compassionate dad, still reading the sports section.

This, of course, didn't do much to comfort the boy. He began crying more. The dad shook his head and rolled his eyes.

"You just need to quit crying," he finally said, then ignored the boy for the rest of the time.

Uninvolved-style parents are more apt to ignore their children's emotional responses. They don't get involved in the emotional worlds of their kids, either because they don't care or because they are uncomfortable with feelings. Children raised by these parents either give up or else they try harder than ever to get an emotional reaction out of their parents. Often we see these kids become more coercive and manipulative with their emotions, working desperately to get their parents to respond to them.

As an aside, my own daughter got sand in her eye at the park some months later, so I made sure that I gave her a good amount of care and attention lest some other child psychologist nearby was collecting material for a book.

4. Inconsistent Style

Imagine this situation: A child and his mom walk into a drugstore to pick up a prescription. On the way to the pharmacy, the boy sees the candy on display.

"Mom, I want some candy."

Mom ignores him.

"Mom, I said I want some candy."

Again, mom ignores him.

"MOM!" he yells, "I want some candy."

Mom's face twists into a scowl. "No!" she says.

"Please . . . " the boy pleads.

Mom smacks him on the arm. "I said 'no.' Didn't you hear me?" she says.

"But please. Just a little bit," he says in his best whiny voice.

Mom just looks away, ignoring him.

A few seconds pass.

"Can I?" he asks again.

"Fine," she says, snatching up some M&M's. "Just be quiet until we get out of here." The boy complies, quiet as a church mouse as they finish waiting.

Inconsistent-style parents are all over the map with their emotions. The same behavior on any given day might get rewarded, punished, or altogether ignored. The children of these parents are typically very persistent in their emotional reactions. They are often willing to risk the consequences because they know they will eventually win out and get what they want. Logic and reason won't work, but that intense, increasingly shrill emotion will. Later in life, expect these kids to grow up to be highly manipulative and coercive.

* * *

Sometimes it is *not* a good idea for parents to help their own child learn emotional control. The child may not want to discuss her feelings with her parents for any number of reasons; she may even have feelings about her parents that she isn't comfortable saying out loud. If this is the case, be sensitive and consult with a professional who might be able to fill this role. Otherwise, this can be a good process between parents and their own children, especially with younger kids.

❑ Cares about the Feelings of Others

My daughter Abbey is one of the most tender-hearted children that I have ever known. This quality makes her incredibly endearing to everyone she knows. Once, when she was only about four years old, she noticed that Ellen was having a hard time with trying to get everyone ready for school. Ellen let out a sigh and Abbey looked up at her and said, "Mom, being a parent is hard." What four-year-old is that emotionally tuned in to notice the meaning of a sigh? That's a rare child!

Most younger children don't give a rip about how other people feel. This isn't because they are selfish brats. It is because *empathy*, the experience of caring about the feelings of others, is a developmental task that is built upon cognitive skills that don't usually develop until a child is about seven years old.

The building block for empathy is *perspective taking*. To care about the feelings of others, you have to first consider that other people have different experiences than you do. Younger kids are so cognitively egocentric that they just assume everyone sees things the way they do. For example, if you asked a preschooler to look at a display of a block, a cylinder, and a pyramid arranged in a certain way, then asked her what it would look like to someone sitting at a different angle, she will almost always choose the picture of what it looks like from her viewpoint. Emotionally, they are the same way. It never occurs to them that other people might have different feelings than they do.

By the age of seven, most children can begin to take perspective more consistently. To develop this, a good exercise to do with kids is to read a story or watch a movie and then talk about things from the perspective of several of the characters. How did he view the situation? How did she feel about what happened? How did he see things differently from her? This practice can be a natural part of reading time or family discussion after a movie.

When a child can take perspective well, he can then begin to develop a greater sense of empathy. It is a two-step process: (1) I *recognize* that she feels sad, (2) I *care* that she is sad. Taking perspective alone is not enough. To be truly empathetic, a child must care about how other people feel.

To help a child improve his empathy, it's wise to make sure you talk about the feelings of other people a lot and about how certain events must have caused another person to feel. You can ask good questions, such as "How do you think Doug felt when his brother had to go into the hospital?" and then follow it up with "And how do you feel about that?" Notice that first you help him recognize the feelings of another, then you ask him to care about that feeling.

It's also important for children to have real-life experiences that help promote empathy, such as visits to the nursing home, a short-term mission or service project to an impoverished country, or volunteer work with Special Olympics. These authentic experiences help empathy become part of the child's life and not just an abstract idea.

❑   Feels Bad after Doing Something Wrong

Gary Hirte killed a man in cold blood by shooting and stabbing him. When asked in an interview about his crime, he said, "There's no reason I should be held accountable for this. That's just the way I feel. I can't change that." When he was younger, he apparently liked to run over animals with his car. He admitted this and said, "I don't have any guilt for killing little animals because I figure I am doing them a favor. It's just the way it's justified in my mind."

I've seen some scary kids in my professional career and one stands out in my mind. Ten-year-old Landon came to see me after he tried to poison his baby brother. At first, he denied it, but when the evidence was too strong to be denied, he simply rolled his eyes and said, "He deserved it." When I asked him what his eighteen-month-old brother did to deserve something like that, he said, "He's annoying."

Kids like Landon often end up in jail. The inability to feel bad about doing something wrong is a frightening thing that leads to trouble. On the other hand, for kids to regret mistakes and harmful actions can protect them against many bad outcomes. It allows them to learn from mistakes, treat people more respectfully, and have better self-control.

The kissing cousin of empathy is *remorse*. A child can care about the feelings of another person but not necessarily feel bad if he does something wrong. Although these concepts are interrelated, remorse may be an even more advanced developmental task. Just as empathy relies on perspective taking, remorse relies on empathy. A child typically cannot feel bad about wrongdoing without caring about others.

Determining what is right or wrong is a fascinating developmental process. A psychologist named Lawrence Kohlberg spent much of his professional life studying how people develop the ability to reason on moral issues. He came up with six stages that individuals seem to go through in progression. The first and lowest stage of moral reasoning is that someone sees something as either right or wrong based on whether they get punished or not. If you get punished, it was bad; if not, it was okay. The second stage is that something is right or wrong based on whether you get something out of it. If it helps you, it was a good thing to do; if not, it wasn't so great. The third stage reasons that something is morally right if that is what a good boy or girl would do. Usually, this means it is good if it pleases someone else. The fourth stage of moral reasoning is that something is right or good based on a rule or a law. If you follow the rules, it is good; if you break the rules, it is bad. The fifth stage is concerned about the greater good. It is good if it benefits the most people or is generally good for society. The final stage reasons that something is morally correct based on whether something is inherently right or wrong. For example, honesty is inherently good, so it must be upheld, regardless of the consequences, whether you get something out of it, or even whether there is a rule or law about it.

To move a child up from lower stages of moral reasoning, you have to expose her to the next stage of moral thinking. For example, if she is operating at stage one, you have to show her how stage two works. She sees something is right or wrong based on whether she gets punished, but you show her that it can be right or wrong based on how it can help her out. Children progress through these stages one at a time. They don't suddenly leap from stage one to stage four. Many parents try to challenge lower levels of moral reasoning with thinking that doesn't make sense to the child. They will say things to a stage one child such as "You can't steal things from your sisters because that hurts the whole family" or "You shouldn't lie because it's always important to be honest." Although these things are true, your child probably won't get the point. If you want your child to move ahead, you'll have to expose her to just the next level of moral reasoning, then on to the next.

Becoming an emotionally intelligent person might take some work, but the long-term rewards are well worth it. Being a person who can talk about emotions openly and honestly, care about the feelings of others, and feel remorse will serve a child in her school, her career, and, most important, in her relationships.

Ashland Library
01/29/07 11:52AM
(606) 329-0090

Checkout Receipt

****

CHECKED OUT TO: CRUM, TABBATHA L.

Prime time : how baby boomers will rev 3
32930015566T1   02/12/07
Parenting the millennial generation : 3
32930025782994   02/12/07

_____

TOTAL: 2

ANY FEE, FINE OR OVERDUE ITEM/S
WILL BLOCK USER'S CARD.
FINE PER BOOK $0.15 A DAY
FINE PER DVD/VIDEO $1.00 A DAY
FINE FOR INTER-LIBRARY LOANS $1.00 A DAY
Thank You

8

Cognitive Protective Factors

When I was in graduate school, I had to learn to give IQ tests by asking friends and acquaintances to volunteer to be my guinea pigs. I lived with three other guys, so I asked one of my roommates, Brit, whether he would let me give him the adult version of the intelligence test. He thought it would be interesting, so he agreed to do it. As I was giving it, I was sure I was doing it wrongly. I was a novice, but I was pretty sure you weren't supposed to be getting *everything* right.

After I scored it, I was even more convinced that I had messed it up. The scores were off the chart on almost every subtest. Sheepishly, I brought in my testing form to my professor and we reviewed it. I was ready to feel like an idiot scoring it incorrectly. However, after we went over it, clearly I had administered it correctly. Brit was just an incredibly intelligent guy. He stopped buying his dental school textbooks after the first semester and still managed to graduate third in his class in one of the most competitive programs in the country. His IQ score was the highest I have ever seen.

It's good to be smart. Being able to think clearly, reason well, and use certain cognitive strengths benefits people in countless ways. Intelligence opens up doors in life and helps a person achieve success. It lets a person learn about the world, chart a course for the future, or sail through dental school without cracking a book.

Our research found four cognitive factors that serve as protective factors for children: possessing solid intelligence, being able to come up with solutions to problems in life, believing that good choices lead to good results, and having positive and realistic goals for the future.

❑   Has Average or Better than Average Intelligence

The concept of intelligence has been a hot topic, especially over the past decade. Some people have suggested that different racial and ethnic groups have different intellectual abilities, setting off intense debates. Others have argued that standardized intelligence tests are not valid; we really don't know what intelligence is, so we surely can't measure it.

Another concept that has generated a lot of discussion is the notion that there are many forms of intelligence.

More than a decade ago, Harvard professor Howard Gardner published a book entitled *Multiple Intelligences*, which suggested that traditional ideas about intelligence were too limited and thus overlooked the broader range of some children's potential. Gardner proposed that there were eight different forms of intelligence that should be considered for each child:

- *Linguistic intelligence*—Children with this type of intelligence are especially good with understanding and using words.
- *Logical-mathematical intelligence*—Kids who have this kind of intelligence are great with reasoning, especially with numbers.
- *Spatial intelligence*—Children with this type of intelligence can understand how things are related to each other in three dimensions.
- *Bodily-kinesthetic intelligence*—These are the children who have a tremendous awareness of their body, how it moves, and how to control it. They are often talented dancers or athletes.
- *Musical intelligence*—These children have a high degree of musical aptitude in performing, composing, or understanding music.
- *Interpersonal intelligence*—These are the highly socially skilled kids. They have great ability to read others and understand new social situations.
- *Intrapersonal intelligence*—These are the emotionally intelligent and self-aware children.
- *Naturalistic intelligence*—These are the children who are tuned into aspects of nature, animals, and even cultural artifacts.

Gardner's theory has been both widely embraced and criticized. Those who support his concept of intelligence say it allows parents and educators to look at kids as having different abilities that shouldn't be minimized or neglected. Those who criticize it say that it so broadens the concept of intelligence that the word "intelligence" loses any real meaning. To be honest, I tend to land more on the side of those who are critical of this way of thinking about intelligence. Reasonable people can differ on this idea, but Gardner's theory seems borne out of an era when it was unacceptable to say that a child simply was not smart. If he wasn't intellectually smart, it was politically correct to say he was "music smart" or "body smart," and so on. I don't dispute the fact that these other abilities exist and are important, but I hesitate to call them intelligences. I do accept the tenet of "intrapersonal intelligence" or emotional intelligence because there is compelling research to support that construct. However, the other seven "multiple intelligences" appear to me to be either talents, abilities, or components of intellectual intelligence.

Why go to all the trouble of discussing Gardner's theory only to disagree with it? Because you need to be aware of what is being said about intelligence. You may hear educators or other professionals say things such as "He's got more of a social intelligence than book smarts." When they say things like this they are essentially saying, "He's not very bright, but he's polite and friendly." I'm not minimizing the importance of having good social skills. It's one of the social protective factors. I am just making the point that this particular protective factor refers to cognitive ability—sheer intellectual firepower—and not musical talents, athleticism, or social skills.

This protective factor is simply the flip side of its risk factor. Low intelligence is a risk factor that places it in the minus column, whereas average or better than average intelligence is in the plus column. The average IQ score is 100, with scores of 90 to 110 making up the Average range. Scores of 111 to 119 make up the High Average range, scores from 120 to 129 are in the Superior range, and scores of 130 and above are called Very Superior. There is no category after that. People frequently ask me, "What is the IQ score for genius?" The answer is that there is no such designation, at least not according to the IQ tests. The word "genius" is not in the intelligence test vocabulary.

On the other side of average, IQ scores from 80 to 89 are called Low Average, and scores from 70 to 79 are called Borderline. Scores below 70 are in the Mentally Handicapped range. To put it into perspective, a score of 69 puts someone in the 2nd percentile among other people the same age. In other words, if 100 people were selected at random and put in order from most intelligent to least intelligent, an individual with this low an IQ would be ninety-eighth in line.

Though I ultimately disagree with Gardner's concept of multiple intelligences, it's important to point out that intelligence is not a unitary trait. That is, it has more than one aspect to it. Intelligence appears to include such things as verbal comprehension, visual reasoning, memory, processing speed, and possibly some other traits. Most tests produce a measure of overall intelligence, called a Full Scale IQ score or General Intellectual Ability score, but they also tell you important information about a person's pattern of cognitive strengths and weaknesses. One of the cool things about IQ tests is that they don't just give you one big score, they give you a good profile about how a person's brain works and how that person can learn best.

The final part of actually making a choice is the easiest. In truth, if you can get a kid to generate options before making a decision, you've cleared the high hurdle. Kids tend to make a choice from an option menu more easily than generating possibilities in the first place. Obviously, most kids—and many adults—don't think through options well. It is a skill that must be practiced in order to be useful.

Cognitive skills, such as problem-solving skills, are similar to physical skills. Some people are naturally gifted athletes; the rest of us have to practice to get good. I've known kids who have ridden their bikes without training wheels on their second try, but most require several attempts with a lot of spills. Similarly, some people are just naturally good decision makers, whereas other people need to practice decision-making skills a number of times, fail miserably on occasion, then get better over time. The person who gives up on the bike will never learn to ride it; the one who gives up practicing cognitive skills won't learn them either. As a parent, you can help your children learn these skills by practice, practice, practice.

❑ Believes Good Choices Lead to Good Results

A fourteen-year-old girl was preparing to go out on the mat for her floor exercises in the gymnastics final. She was deep in concentration, not looking at the other competitors, just in her own zone. Before she stepped out, someone from the crowd yelled, "Good luck, Kim!"

Kim looked straight ahead, but muttered under her breath to her coach, "I make my own luck." The coach smiled knowingly, fully aware that he was the one who had taught her that line. Not surprisingly, Kim nailed the routine and left the floor with a smile on her face and a winking acknowledgment to her coach. "Make your own luck" had become one of the team sayings.

Children who really believe this statement are more likely to nail the routine, ace the test, or learn to control their behavior. Those who don't believe that we make our own luck don't tend to do as well. What I'm describing is a concept called *locus of control*.

I once started telling a kid about locus of control during a therapy session. As I continued my little lesson, he interrupted me and asked, "Why is it called locust of control?" I had to explain that it was locus, not locust the bug, and it meant "center of," or the place where something happens. In this case, locus of control refers to whether the cause of something in a person's life is internal or external.

People with an external locus of control tend to think that things just happen to them because of factors outside of themselves, such as environmental or situational variables. These folks are much more likely to think outcomes are the result of good or bad luck rather than the product of effort or, in some cases, lack of effort.

The most interesting thing about locus of control is that it is not the reality of whether things happen by chance or by hard work that seems to make a difference in a person's life. It is the *belief* about these things that makes the difference. People with an external locus of control live like that's true, not seeing the point of hard work and determination, believing that randomness is the norm. Consequently, these people—both kids and adults—are likely to give up more easily, don't achieve as much, and are prone to blame others or circumstances for their misfortunes. Children with an external locus of control are more likely to get depressed or feel anxious and have more behavioral problems.

In contrast, people who have an internal locus of control believe that they control their own destiny by their actions. Good actions and decisions usually lead to good outcomes, according to those with an internal locus of control. Like Kim, children with a more internal locus of control believe they make their own luck, and as a result, they do.

Can you help your child develop a more internal locus of control? The answer is yes. Here are four practical ways that you can nurture this process.

1. Be Consistent

Research has found that parents who are more consistent in their responses to their children tend to produce kids with a more internal sense of control. Of course, this makes perfect sense. If there is a clear connection between what you do—either good or bad—and the response that you get, it follows that you will see that the world tends to operate in a logical, cause-and-effect way. This leads to a greater sense of healthy personal control. You don't have to be perfectly consistent, but your child's experience should be that you do what you say and you follow through on what you promise.

A key to being consistent is to set expectations ahead of time. In every situation, your child should know what the expectations are. These should be fair and developmentally appropriate. Consequences should be given consistently, as should reinforcers and rewards. Lisa Whelchel has written a great book, *Creative Correction,* that gives wonderfully practical examples of both corrections and rewards. Here's one that we use: if we observe our girls playing well together or doing something spontaneously kind or helpful, we give them a "Caught ya being good" reward. Sometimes this is an extra dollar of allowance, a later bedtime to watch a TV show, or a trip to Dairy Queen. These little surprises are always random and never expected. Despite the intentional "inconsistency," this practice is in the context of a fairly consistent world for our kids.

Consistency produces feelings of safety in children, helps them develop better cause-and-effect thinking, and gives them a greater sense of personal control. It's an important part of being a good parent. If you struggle with being consistent with your kids, spend time thinking through obstacles that keep you from achieving consistency. Write them down and begin to problem solve how to remove those obstacles one at a time. For example, if you are too tired to follow through on your rules and limits, brainstorm about how to correct for this. If you and your spouse are not aligned, then begin the dialogue about how to get on the same page.

2. Encourage Independence

If you've ever observed parents of toddlers, you can often pick out the nervous, overprotective ones in a matter of minutes. They don't let their children explore too much. They are constantly hypervigilant and don't seem the least bit relaxed around their kids. Skip ahead a few years and these folks are usually still doing the same thing. They are eager to shelter their kids from bad influences and bad consequences.

Parents running interference for their children by blocking the school's attempt to enforce penalties is such a widespread practice that *Time* magazine ran a cover story about it. In interviews, nearly all the teachers I spoke with told me stories of how parents come to the rescue of their child by protesting grades or defending "their little precious" against consequences they deem unfair. A sixth grade teacher told me, "I don't think there is a week that goes by where I don't have some angry parent telling me how unfair some punishment was for their child. And I'm not talking about anything severe. I'm talking about having to sit quietly at lunch for being disruptive in class." Parents who do this send a clear message that reinforces dependent behavior at best and irresponsible behavior at worst. Your child will have a hard time developing an internal sense of control if you support his belief that he is the victim of mistreatment, especially where none exists. Remember that children with an external locus of control see outside forces and bad luck as factors that cause things to happen.

Perhaps the parents who are most prone to feel like their child is being persecuted need to examine their own locus of control.

If your child is overly dependent or irresponsible, take a step back and examine why this might be. Some kids act this way because of temperamental issues or emotional difficulties. However, it may be worth considering whether you have reinforced this behavior in any way. If you are being overprotective by not allowing your children to fail, then consider how you can change your own attitudes and actions. Having overprotective parents leads to lower levels of educational attainment in kids and longer-than-average time to finish their schooling. In the short term, it may seem like you are doing them a favor by completing their chores for them, complaining to the principal, or helping them write the paper the night before it is due, but in the long run, you are probably doing them a serious injustice.

If you want your child to have a greater sense of personal control and power in her own life, then you would be wise to promote independence. Let your child explore and take risks that are reasonably safe and age-appropriate. It's equally important to let your child fail at times. If your kid wants a pet and agrees to be responsible for it, then hold her to it. If it doesn't happen, you should *not* step in and start taking care of the hamster. Instead, call a family meeting and make it clear that she has to take care of the pet or it has to go. We learn as much from our failures as from our successes. Your mission is not to make sure your child never fails. Rather, it is to help him learn how to be responsible and increasingly independent.

3. Make Positive Attributions

A few years back, I had an interesting discussion with a high school senior about locus of control. He was an incredibly smart boy who liked to think things through intellectually. He said that people develop a more internal sense of control based on what happens to them. People who have had lots of bad things happen in their lives have a more external sense of control, whereas people who have had good and easy lives are likely to have a more internal sense of control. His mother had committed suicide and he was rejected by other kids throughout school, so he had a more external sense of control, he reasoned. I told him that this made sense, but that years of research had found the opposite to be true. People could have soft lives and be very external and others could have lots of hard things happen to them and have an internal sense of control. How we think about those events, and beyond this how we think about ourselves, is ultimately more important.

How people think about themselves can be shaped by a process called *attribution*. This refers to the practice of attributing a quality or skill to a person. For example, if I say to my daughter, "You are a very fast runner," (which she is, by the way), then I am making an attribution. Making attributions can be powerful and can help shape a child's sense of control.

A couple of studies show how attributions work with kids. In the first study, a group of researchers visited a fifth grade class and handed out candy during recess. Afterwards, they counted how many candy wrappers were left on the playground and how many made it to the trashcan. Of course, the ground won. Over the next couple of weeks, the researchers coached members of the school staff to make comments to the class. During a drop-in visit, the principal remarked about how neat their classroom looked and how much they must care about keeping things clean. The custodian wrote a note on the board telling them that they had the neatest room in the school and how they must all be very neat students. Finally, the teacher would make similar comments about how neat the room was and how neat the children were. When the researchers came back a second time to hand out more candy during recess, there was a big improvement in their littering behavior. The trashcan ended up with more wrappers than the ground. At the beginning of the study, only 15 percent of the wrappers landed in the trash, but by the end, 80 percent of the trash was properly disposed of.

What is remarkable about this little study is what the researchers did not do. They didn't model any behavior; they didn't reward or punish any behavior; they didn't even make an argument for or against a certain behavior. In fact, in another classroom, they had the adults try to persuade the children not to litter. Despite the good lectures, those children did not change their littering behavior much. At the end of the study, only 40 percent of the candy wrappers were put in the trash, exactly half the percentage for the attribution group. Attempts at direct persuasion were clearly not as successful.

Instead, what did work was attributing a certain behavior and characteristic to the kids. Whenever they heard someone compliment them on having a neat room, the children probably had a little internal dialogue in their heads that made them ask, "Why is the room neat and clean?" They had to answer, "We are neat and clean kids, so we pick up after ourselves." Dr. Steve Booth-Butterfield, who teaches a class in persuasion theory at the University of West Virginia, says about this study, "In other words, the children made internal attributions. And if you believe that you are the kind of person who is neat and does not litter, what happens when you have a candy wrapper? That's right, you throw it away in the waste can." And in this study, that's exactly what happened. That is the power of attributions.

Another study that Dr. Booth-Butterfield uses in his class shows the power of attributions in improving a child's school achievement. A bunch of second graders who were learning math were assigned to one of three groups. In each group, the teachers had to follow scripted lines when interacting with their students. In the first group, the teachers tried to *attribute* certain skills or qualities to their kids with such phrases as "You really seem to know your math assignments well" and "You really work hard on your math." In the second group, the teachers tried to *persuade* their students with such phrases as "You should be getting better grades on your math work." The final group had teachers trying to *reinforce* their students by saying things such as "I'm really proud of your good work" and "You made excellent progress." At the end of the study, the kids were all assessed. Each group showed improvements in self-esteem, but the attribution group had the greatest improvement. Equally important was that the kids in the attribution group showed greater improvements on their math tests and kept those gains for longer than either of the other two groups.

I use attributions all the time in therapy. I tell my clients such things as "You seem to be a person who wants to treat other people right" or "You're the kind of person who can work hard to dig your way out of a discouraging situation." Many good parents do this unwittingly when they say, "You are so good at helping around the house" or "I really like how you work so hard in school," for example. Those are attributions. Bear in mind that this is not the same as flattery. Flattery is insincere and usually false. Attributions involve noticing something about a person or her behavior and attributing it to who they are as a person. "You are the smartest kid in your school" is flattery; "You are a really smart kid" is an attribution.

As a parent, you can use attributions well, especially if you do so sparingly and sincerely. One of the secrets to this approach is to say less than you want to say. For example, you might be tempted to say something like "You are really helpful with the dog. As you are so helpful, it would be good for you to make sure you walk him and make sure he has water in his bowl every day." See how this crosses the line from attribution to persuasion? If you said, "You are great at helping me clear the table. If you do that every night this week, I'll let you rent a video this weekend," it would cross into reinforcement. Attributions are simple, and they let the other person do the work. You say, "You really have some great skills with your artwork," and let them do the rest.

4. Develop Delay of Gratification

Stanford University has been home to some of the most creative psychology research ever done. In one study, four-year-old kids were told to stay in a room and wait for the adult to return. On a plate in front of them was a yummy marshmallow. Mmmmm. Enough to tempt any red-blooded four-year-old. But there was a twist: before the grown-up left the room, she told the child that if he waited until she returned, he could have *two* yummy marshmallows. The adult left the room and there sat the child, staring that fluffy white goodness in the face. Some of them waited for a while, but finally gave in and gobbled up the treat; other kids snatched it up before the grown-up had gotten out of the room! However, there were some kids who waited—probably with bouncing legs and gritted teeth, but still they waited. More than a decade later, the children who were able to wait scored, on average, more than 200 points higher on the SATs than their peers who gave in.

Some children know how to wait for something they want. They save up allowance or wait until their birthday or work hard now for grades later. Other kids have a hard time saying no to themselves. If they want it, they take it. They tend to trade the future for the present every time, usually with negative long-term results.

Psychologists call this ability to say no to the present temptation and wait for something better *delay of gratification*. This is an emotional skill that is nearly absent at birth but begins to develop during the preschool years. Kids who are good at delay of gratification often do well in many aspects of their lives because it helps them develop a greater sense of internal control.

You can build your child's ability to delay gratification by creating situations where he can practice. You might say something like "If you don't spend your allowance this weekend, I'll give you an extra dollar as a bonus for waiting." I know one dad who set up a clever experiment. He told his younger daughters that he would give them a penny on the first day, then double the amount every day for up to nine days: two cents on day two, four cents on day three, and so on. It doesn't sound like much? By the ninth day, you are making more than five dollars. If the offer continued to the end of the second week, you could bank $163.83. Guess how much money you make by the end of the month? Do the math yourself. It will shock you. The girls could get their money at any point in the nine-day period if they asked for it. He even tempted them with little things such as going to the convenience store to buy some candy. Not surprisingly, after the girls figured it out, they both waited until the end of the nine days to cash in. The point of the exercise was clear: it's good to say no to something *now* in order to get something better *later*. Be creative and see whether you can come up with ways to help your child learn better delay of gratification.

* * *

There are many practical steps that you can take to help your child have a more internal locus of control. Be consistent. Encourage healthy independence. Make positive attributions. Develop the ability to delay gratification. Oh, and one more thing: have an internal sense of control yourself. Your words and actions will only ring true if you look at the world this way yourself.

❑   Has Positive and Realistic Goals for the Future

When I was a little kid, I used to have a blue tricycle with a rounded windshield that had the word "Police" on it. I pedaled it around the neighborhood and told everyone that I was Officer Dave Davis. Why I decided to change my last name, I really couldn't tell you, but I was pretty committed to being a cop. Somewhere before middle school, my career in law enforcement was jettisoned in favor of my new vocation: cartoonist. Copying from *Mad* magazine, I did a dead-on imitation of Don Martin's style of drawing. If anyone ever had need of a cheap imitation of the guy in a propeller beanie getting cracked in the head with a baseball, I was their man. By high school, the cartooning gave way to my desire to pursue a newfound passion for radio. In college I actually had the chance to work in a few radio stations, including on-air shifts and voiceover work for commercials. It was just enough experience to let me know that I would rather have a sharp stick in my eye than work in radio all my life. Faced with the prospect of having to choose a new major, I picked psychology—and here we are!

I share all this semi-embarrassing information about my early career trajectory to make a simple point. It is better to have goals than not to have them. With goals, you are at least moving forward toward something. Even if you change your goals—which most of us do as we mature—it is more about the process of setting realistic goals than it is about the specific goal itself.

It pains me when I see kids, especially teenagers, who have no clue about what they might like to pursue. When you asked them, you get a lot of shrugged shoulders. Perhaps it wouldn't surprise you to know that a good many of these kids smoke marijuana on a fairly frequent basis. But there are also some drug-free kids who have no sense of future direction. When you aren't moving forward, it's hard to get motivated to do the difficult things now—especially school—that will get you closer to your goal.

The other extreme also concerns me. Frankly, I don't enjoy conversations with kids who are convinced they will be the next Daniel Radcliffe (a.k.a. Harry Potter), the next Michael Jordan, or the next John Mayer, despite mediocre talent as an actor, athlete, or musician. Adults tend to fall into one of two camps on this issue. The first camp says encourage any passion; don't throw cold water on their dreams. The second camp says that these kids need a good dose of reality. I am closer to the second camp. I've seen kids who were fully capable of being accomplished athletes or performers and who are willing to work at it, so I have no problem encouraging them in their pursuits. But there is no good payoff for supporting a kid's goal when she lacks the talent, work ethic, or drive to make it happen. For those kids, I always tell them that it's good to come up with more than one goal and then I challenge them to produce a list of at least five things that they could do.

How does a kid determine what his long-term goals should be? I would argue that it is where the three circles in Figure 2 overlap: passion, talent, and benefit.

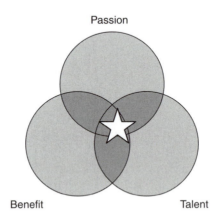

Figure 2

A person's passion is his love, his delight. It is the thing that gives him pleasure when he thinks about it or does it. Talent is obviously skill or ability. Benefit refers to whether the pursuit is worthwhile, whether it meets some need or contributes something significant to others or is an inherently valuable, beneficial venture. If a person loves basketball but doesn't have enough talent to pursue it as a career, then that probably isn't the best goal. If a person is a talented musician but has no passion for it, then he should pick something else to pursue as a career. Also, if a person has great aim and a desire to be a mafia hitman, which isn't universally beneficial, then that's probably not the best way to go.

A person should work toward something that she loves, that she could be good at, and that is a worthy goal. Assuming that an individual has the requisite amount of passion and talent, the possibilities are nearly endless in careers ranging from the arts, sciences, and education to financial services, law, medicine, social services, law enforcement, and countless others.

Many parents push their kids to do something that is safe and conventional. They want their kids to get a business or engineering degree, for example. That's fine, but if someone pursues a career because of external pressure, then it will either fail or the kid may feel locked into a job that he doesn't enjoy. Some kids are pretty unconventional and it's often a good idea for parents to acknowledge this rather than try to make them be something that they are not. I don't know about you, but I want my kids to land in jobs they love. If someone came up to me and said I had two choices, either quit my job and take another job making double my current income or keep my job but take a 50 percent pay cut, then I'd have to keep my job and tighten our budget.

Helping your kid set long-term goals is a process that may span months or years. I would suggest having ongoing conversations about her interests. What does she really enjoy? What does she like to think about for fun? From there, I would observe her and make mental notes about her level of skill in certain areas, including academic subjects, hobbies, and extracurricular activities. I'd then start some conversations about what I have heard and seen, such as "You said that you really like your science class and I've noticed that you are really good in math." Begin planting those attributions and keep the dialogue open. Remember that a child's goals and career aspirations will likely switch several times, but it's the desire and ability to set those goals that is most important.

As kids get older, there is no substitute for actual hands-on experience to help shape up their goals. If I had had the chance in high school to work in a radio station even for a summer, I would not have spent a year of college as a communications major. However, the opposite has been true for others whom I have known. They did a summer internship in a radio or TV station and they were instantly hooked. There is a private school in our city that requires all of its graduating seniors to spend the last two weeks of their academic year in a full-time internship. Not only is this the best cure for senior-itis that I've ever seen, it also allows them to explore career interests by shadowing a professional and experiencing a real-life job. We've had a couple of their kids intern at our practice, and even though they can't do actual clinical practice ("Here, Johnny, give this IQ test!"), they can do research, observe in-service trainings, and take on some special projects. These kinds of experiences either scare people away from a profession or solidify their career paths. If your older child wants to be a vet, I'd explore helping them get a job or even an unpaid internship at an animal clinic. If he wants to start his own business when he gets older, call a friend who has done it and see if your boy can hang around the shop for a few days.

This is a good idea even with unmotivated kids. I tell parents that I can help kids with a lot of things, but I can't make them want to do something they don't want to do. Talking, even using motivational approaches, usually can't create passion where none exists. However, if a kid sees something in action it can ignite a fire that wasn't there before. Encourage your kids to get involved and try out some things. They may fall in love with a career that will bring them tremendous pleasure for years to come.

9

Academic Protective Factors

Collinswood Dual Language Academy sits among a neighborhood of tiny houses, hidden in the middle of Charlotte. It's a brick building with a few modular classrooms out back. There's a flowering tree in the front and some nice landscaping, but you can still tell it's an older building that isn't as impressive as some of the newer elementary schools in town. However, if you spend any time inside, you will sense something exciting going on there. With a campus full of native Spanish speakers and native English speakers, you hear the chatter of two languages in the hallways during class transitions.

In a city that has increased its Hispanic population by 600 percent in the past decade, such a school is essential, but what is amazing is that it takes its mission so seriously and does it so well. Collinswood is a school that cares for its staff and students. It has high educational and academic standards, yet it is willing to individualize it approach to help every child succeed. This philosophy pays off; it's one of the highest-performing schools in the entire city. It's the only school that has no gap between the test scores of students representing different racial or ethnic groups or socioeconomic backgrounds.

Collinswood is the first dual language immersion school in North Carolina, and it has become a model for other schools systems around the country that want to develop dual language programs. Collinswood's principal, Maria Petrea, has been widely credited with helping the school become a place of excellence. She has intentionally hired staff from various countries, some coming to the United States just to work at the school. Her philosophy is that the diversity of the staff and student body make the educational experience richer for everyone. She says, "Collinswood has more to offer than high test scores. The blending of the Latino/Hispanic and American cultures creates a diverse school community where appreciation for all is represented. The richness of each culture enhances our own."

By the time they leave Collinswood, most students will be able to understand, speak, and write proficiently both English and Spanish. The majority of students perform at or above grade level in both languages. In addition to this, Ms. Petrea can list at least ten other benefits of language immersion, including improvements in self-esteem and better problem-solving skills.

All of this nestles in an old brick building hidden in an old neighborhood in the middle of a big city. I know there are hundreds of other excellent schools just like it hidden in neighborhoods across the country. Struggling schools with drugs and guns make the news, but schools such as Collinswood make the lives of our kids better and brighter every day.

When you are a kid, school is second only to family as the most important thing in your life. During most of the year, it is what consumes the majority of your waking hours. Being a good student and going to a good school are extraordinarily important. In our research, we found four academic protective factors that can improve the lives of children and give them a better future.

❏ Is a Good Overall Student

Not long ago, I read a story of a high school dropout who went on to become a self-made millionaire by making shrewd real estate deals. Certainly, we have all heard heartwarming stories of people who dropped out of school and then became bazillionaires by the time they were thirty, but the reason those individuals catch our attention is because they are anomalies. They are not the norm. Education is critical for success in our culture. It's no surprise to learn that a person's earning potential is directly related to her level of education. Figure 3 illustrates average lifetime earnings based on education: the higher the degree, the more money she

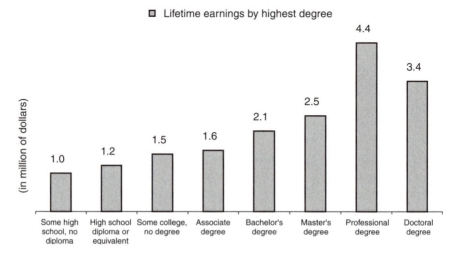

Figure 3

can expect to make. Since many people with doctoral degrees end up teaching or doing research, their lifetime earning potential might not be as high as that of those who have an MBA, a JD, or some other professional degree, but there is a clear relationship between having more education and making more money.

In addition to the obvious relationship between education and money, there are other aspects of education that help children tremendously, both now and in later life. Here's just a partial list of some of the benefits of more education.

Benefits of education beginning in childhood

- Better decision-making skills
- More enjoyment of hobbies and leisure time
- More open-minded
- More cultured
- More consistent
- Less authoritarian
- Less prejudice
- Greater knowledge of national and world affairs
- Better physical health
- More optimistic view of future potential

Benefits of education in adulthood

- Better financial sensibility
- Improved quality of life for their children
- Greater professional and personal mobility
- Greater job security
- Enhanced social status
- Healthier children
- Tendency to spend more time with their children
- Better preparation of own children for higher education
- Greater workplace productivity

Being a good student unlocks much more than the ability to make more money. Children and teens who make education a priority are investing in their future quality of life and ultimately in the lives of their own children.

Unfortunately, there are many kids who are not good students, either because of cognitive limitations, learning or attention problems, emotional or behavioral difficulties, or some other reason. Often parents battle their unmotivated or low-achieving children over school performance. As important as school is, consider whether it is wise to do battle over academics. Some kids do need extra pressure to do their best in school, but for others you can end up harming your relationship and not having much to show for it at the end. As with most aspects of parenting, this calls for wisdom. Just because education is important doesn't necessarily mean that you need to duke it out when the grades are low or she seems to be slacking off.

For kids who are good students, just clear a path and let them do their thing. Make sure they are in a good school that is challenging but not overwhelming. Keep encouraging them and letting them know that you see how good a job they are doing. It also might be wise to do a learning styles inventory or some other type of cognitive testing so they know how they learn best in order to maximize their study time.

For other kids who are struggling (or maybe aren't struggling enough), you may want to spend more of your energy trying to find a school setting that fits them best. I've seen lots of mediocre students thrive in better school situations. However, if you've tried goading and rewarding and lecturing and everything else and nothing works, then make sure you still work hard to keep a solid relationship with your child. I've seen too many parents who were so upset by the academic underperformance of their kid that they argued and fought almost constantly. Usually the result is that these parents end up having a poor relationship with their child and he still doesn't do well in school. Don't fall into that trap. Work hard to let him do his best in school, but if he falls short, don't let it cost you the relationship.

❑   Reads at or above Grade Level

Ellen has been the chairperson of the book fair at our school for several years. One year the theme was "Read a Great Tale," so we went out to the school during the weekend and chalked up the walkways with paw prints and long-tailed animals. The kids got off the buses and hopped along the paw prints and giggled at the animals and their tails. Later that week at the book fair, the gym buzzed with excited kids who wanted to buy books to read just for fun.

This generation likes to read. They've been read to since they were young and they have developed a love for reading. When I was younger, there wasn't a single bookstore in my town that had a separate kids section, but now there are half a dozen megastores nearby that have big sections that are about the size of my house devoted to young readers (okay, I exaggerate, but they are big).

Reading greatly benefits a child by improving language and speech development, enhancing vocabulary, stirring imagination and creativity, and expanding her fund of knowledge about the world. There are lifelong benefits of reading, too, such as increased confidence, easier acquisition of knowledge, a greater range of interests, and critical-thinking skills. It's a great activity that kids can enjoy for the rest of their lives.

Like many skills, reading is something that can be improved upon over time. A poor reader can become a fair reader and a good reader can become an excellent reader. As a parent, here are four things you can do to improve your child's reading.

1. Emphasize Reading to Learn

Parents may be highly involved with their child's reading in the early years, but once the child gets the basics down, the grown-ups often assume that the hard part is over. However, that's where it really should begin. The real work is helping a child take those basic skills and translate reading into a life skill. Dr. Guy Arcuri, a literacy professor at High Point University, says, "Parents tend to believe that once the child has 'learned to read' at the elementary level, the proverbial 'reading to learn' will follow naturally. You don't want to send the message to the child that reading is more about decoding of letters and words into proper pronunciation than an act of comprehension with a communicative goal in mind."

It's important that kids not just read, but read for the right reasons. When children are younger, it's a good idea to ask them what details they remember about a story. When they get older, it's good to ask them about the main themes in the story. Some parents make reading fun for their younger children by playing games such as "I'm going to read this story and afterward, I want you to tell me how many animals you remember from it and what they did." With older kids, you might want to consider reinforcing or rewarding good reading habits. I know one dad who tells his middle school son that if he reads a book of history or some other work of nonfiction and then sits down and tells the dad what he learned, then he'll pay the boy for teaching him something new. I love hearing things like that.

Don't just make sure your kid has the mechanics of reading down and then assume the rest will naturally follow. Teach your child how to read to learn. More than that, teach her how to love to read.

2. Teach How to Read Actively

A review of the research suggests that one of the keys to improving reading skill is to be an *active reader*. Some people think of reading as a passive process, but it's far from it. The best readers seem to engage with the material in a way that poor readers do not. The good readers think about what the author is trying to say, concentrate during the tough sections, and start thinking of applications to their own life and experience.

A good reader is clear about *why* he is reading. This may sound obvious, but it is a little more complex than you may realize. Think for a moment about how you have been reading this book. Some of you will read every word (bless you!); others will read most of it, but skip some of the illustrations or summary paragraphs; others of you will read just the major chapter headings until you get the main idea. Those of you who read all of it (including the illustrations) are probably reading at least partly for pleasure. You intuitively know that the stories serve only to make the content more enjoyable. Those of you who read most but skipped the stories and summaries are probably reading for specific and helpful information that you can apply to your parenting. Those of you who skimmed just wanted to get the main idea of the book. If you read only the headers and skimmed the rest, but were looking for lots of specific information, then your style was a mismatch with your goal. Knowing why you are reading something ahead of time helps you become a good reader.

3. Work on Reading Speed

When I was younger, I remember a comedian talking about the Evelyn Wood Speed Reading course. "Who is this Evelyn Wood?" the comic asked. He imagined that she was a giant eyeball with an insatiable thirst for books, yelling at all her minions to bring her more pages to read. The point of his monologue was that reading fast was of dubious importance.

Reading speed is not the most important thing, but it is a valuable aspect of being a good reader. Most people can double their reading speed and still have the same level of comprehension. Most educated adults, for example, read around 300 words a minute, but they can get to 600 words a minute with a little work. The same is true for children. The average rates are slower, but the same process applies. The benefit of reading speed is that you can devour more books in a shorter amount of time. As a result, it exposes you to more information about the world and different perspectives on life.

People who want to improve their reading speed can do so if they are willing to try some new techniques and practice them regularly. Researchers have uncovered a few habits that can help a person read faster. First, forget about pronouncing the words as you read them. If you move your throat even slightly or whisper while you read, you'll go slower. You'll be able to read at least twice as fast silently than if you read out loud. Another habit that tends to slow you down is the process of rereading. The research on reading says that the slowest readers are more prone to reread. They go back over what they have read and their pace gets bogged down. It is possible that the reason why slower readers reread more is precisely because they are slow. In other words, since they are slow, their minds wander more, they concentrate more poorly, and then they have to go back over their tracks again because they weren't paying attention. That's one of the reasons why a faster reading pace tends to help—or at least not hurt—comprehension and retention. Finally, the reading experts suggest that you start training yourself to look at phrases rather than reading word for word. This last habit takes lots of practice and is often not a possibility for early readers, but it can be developed as reading skills progress.

Readers have to learn to adjust their reading rate based on the content and difficulty of the material, as well. Stronger readers know that there are times when you can speed up and other times when you need to slow down, much in the same way that car drivers have to adjust for curves, straightaways, and treacherous weather. Here are some guidelines that can help. First, slow down when you are reading unfamiliar words or concepts. Keep going slowly if you are reading difficult sentence structure, highly technical material, or lots of specific details. In contrast, you can change into fourth gear when you come across unnecessary examples or elaborations you don't need in order to get to the point.

4. Assess and Remediate When Needed

What do you do if your child is reading below grade level? Well, the first thing is don't freak out. Grade level scores compare kids with each other, which means that there have to be kids who are reading above and below average. With some intensive effort to increase reading skills, most children can close the gap fairly rapidly. However, if your child is lagging behind and her teachers seem concerned, here are some things to do. First, pursue testing to see whether she might have a learning disability. The way we assess a disability is to compare a child's actual learning with her measured mental ability. We measure mental ability by using IQ tests, which give us information about cognitive firepower. The child's cognitive ability is then compared with how much she has learned in a certain subject area, such as reading, math, or writing, as determined by standardized achievement tests. If a significant gap exists between a child's ability (IQ) and her achievement, then there might be a learning disability. The gap needs to be at least 15 points, but some states use different cutoffs or entirely different formulas.

Using the 15-point discrepancy, you can see that if a child has an IQ score of 100, but gets a score of 82 on reading, then this 18-point gap looks like a learning disability. The reason why 15 points was chosen is that this is the level at which statistically the gap is unlikely to happen by chance, test error, a bad day, or for reasons other than having a real problem in that subject area.

My analogy is that IQ is like a fish tank and achievement is how full it is. If a person has a 100 gallon fish tank, then she can hold 100 gallons. Rarely will she hold 115 gallons, but when she does, we call her an overachiever. When she only has 85 gallons, then we usually say she has a learning disability.

The helpful thing about testing is that the better evaluations will look at different aspects of reading. Psychologists will often use tests that involve sight-word reading, silent reading, out-loud reading, reading speed, overall fluency, and comprehension. Even if a child does not have a learning disability, the process of testing can help pinpoint areas of strength or concern. For example, an evaluation might say that your child can attack new words well, but does it very slowly and has trouble with understanding what the words and sentences mean. Or it might say that she has great comprehension and speed but poor word attack skills, just skipping past words that she doesn't know and figuring it all out in context.

A second thing that I would do if my child were having trouble reading is make sure that she is getting some special attention to her reading either during or after school from a learning specialist or a really skilled tutor. The research shows that children make huge advances when someone helps their reading.

Third, try teaching your child some of the skills mentioned in this section and practice with her. Make it as fun as possible, turning it into a game or even giving some incentives for showing improvement in reading. I know some parents who give points for books or chapters read that can be used later for something special.

Finally, make sure that younger children are being read to every night and older children are reading every night. Like any skill, you can't get good at it without practice. With reading, the more you do it, the better you get. Your comprehension improves, your speed increases, and your enjoyment of it intensifies.

❏ Has a Strong Connection to School

For the past year, I have been interviewing students about their schools. One of the open questions I've asked them was "How do you feel about your school?" Predictably, the responses were all over the map. Some said they loved their school, whereas others couldn't stand it, and still others were just neutral. One boy told me plainly, "It's an awesome school." Another girl was equally blunt when she said, "I think it's a terrible place."

When students feel attached to their school, it is called *school bonding*. A child experiences school bonding when he feels close emotional relationships with those at the school as well as a commitment to the school, including investment in getting good grades and participating in the daily life of the school.

There is an obvious connection between school bonding and academic achievement. The kids who are connected to their schools tend to get better grades overall than kids who are not. This isn't always the case, of course, but it is often true. What is equally important, however, is that kids with a strong interest in school also tend to have less trouble in other areas of their lives. High levels of school bonding have been linked to less drinking, smoking, drug use, delinquency, violence, disruptive behavior, and promiscuity. It's not entirely clear whether school bonding is what causes kids to do better behaviorally or whether it is just that people who have better behavior tend to be better connected to school. There is at least some evidence that the connection with school by itself is part of what promotes prosocial behavior in kids. Whatever the reason, having this strong connection is helpful.

How can you help your kid get better connected to school? First, make sure she's in a school that fits her well. It's hard to be connected to a school where you feel you don't belong. One of my clients, a very creative girl, struggled mightily in school until she transferred to the School of the Arts. From then on, she loved going to school every day. I love going to work every day, but I might not feel so great about going each morning if I worked somewhere else. The same is true for kids. They need to be in an academic setting that fits them well.

I would also suggest encouraging involvement at the school. It's good for your child to have at least one thing that he does at the school:

crossing guard, yearbook staff, baseball player, student council member, cafeteria helper, or something else. It's also good for a parent to be involved with the PTA, book fair, fundraising, or other things. Being involved is one of the best ways to feel connected to school.

Finally, I'd suggest asking a school staff member to serve as a formal or informal mentor for your child if she isn't feeling attached to school. Having a trusted adult—coach, teacher, administrator—take a special interest in your child can help her develop a connection to school in a way that she has not experienced before.

❏ Goes to an Excellent School

What makes a school excellent? I've visited many schools, done training for others, and have interacted with dozens of others around the needs of my clients. I've taken those experiences, along with a review of the research on academic excellence, and I've landed on a few traits that seem to distinguish the best schools. Here are seven qualities of excellent schools.

1. Safety

The best schools are safe, not only physically but emotionally as well. Kids don't have to worry about being hurt during the day in any way. These schools have a good track record of safety and they have fewer episodes of bullying than other schools. The research has found at least five characteristics of schools at which there is less bullying: they encourage and expect parental involvement, they have firm limits for misbehavior, they use nonhostile and nonphysical consequences to deal with misbehavior when it happens, they monitor their students well, and the staff shows positive affection and interest in the students.

Safe schools don't just rely on technology such as cameras and metal detectors. Instead, they have a different culture. The expectations of parents, students, and staff are that people will respect each other. It starts at the top and trickles all the way down. You can read statistics about a particular school, but you will probably have a better sense of the school's culture of safety by visiting it in person. I have been on countless school campuses, and each has its own feel. You can often get a good intuitive sense of whether it would feel safe to be there by taking a tour.

2. Strong Leadership

Like any good organization, good leadership in a school is essential. When we first met Maria Petrea, she said without a hint of arrogance, "I am a very strong principal." Ms. Petrea's strength in leadership is a big reason why her school is so good. She sets the tone, charts the course, and holds people to account. Without her, the school would get by but it wouldn't thrive.

For the past two years, I've carried out extensive research and study on leadership. Some claim that the emphasis on senior leadership in organizations is misguided. However, the more I learn about leadership, the more I realize how important it is to the health of an organization. The tone and culture of an entire organization can be affected by the top leaders. People can feel discouraged and passive or enthused and empowered in their jobs based on the influence of a strong leader. Likewise, the productivity and overall excellence of any organization can be shaped by the people at the top.

When you are considering a school for your child, make sure you meet the principal, headmaster, director, or whoever is the senior leader. Her vision and direction will be a big predictor of how good that school is going to be.

3. Shared Vision

Several of my clients over the years have been excellent athletes. A few of them were ranked as top ten in the state in their sport and went to college as scholarship athletes. One of those guys, a golfer, had played in several state tournaments and was widely considered to be one of the best young golfers in the city. I asked him how he got to be so good and he told me, "You've got to know your game." He explained that you have to know yourself, your strengths and weaknesses, and your plan of attack in order to be an excellent player. He added, "You have to know what you are about when you go out on the course."

If you spend a lot of time in different schools, you'll begin to notice that the really good schools know their game. They know what they are about. They have a clear vision, a mission statement that means something. They know what they do well and what they don't do well. Whether it is being the best in teaching a foreign language, or developing character, or teaching the classics, or helping students fall in love with reading, these schools focus on their strengths. They know what they are trying to accomplish.

Many schools, especially public schools, are expected and pressured to be all things to all people. This is probably a mistake. I support the requirement to serve all students, but every school shouldn't have to do it all. We know from the business literature that organizations with a clear and finely tuned focus tend to do better than those trying to do too many things at once. The same wisdom should be applied to schools. One of the reasons I love magnet or charter schools is they tend to know their game better than others. Even neighborhood public schools can have a clear vision and be truly excellent. Everyone connected to the school should know what the school is about and what they are trying to accomplish.

4. High Standards and Expectations

The best schools have high academic and behavioral expectations and they communicate these clearly to staff, parents, and students. They don't just set lofty goals for their students; they expect good performance and they achieve it. The very best schools manage to do this without smothering kids with work. Some schools confuse high standards with lots of homework. Instead, having excellent instruction, making the most of class time, and giving carefully selected homework assignments will better meet high standards.

When considering a school for your child, see what the school says about itself and its expectations. Then see whether the facts match. Is this school really doing what it sets out to do? Is it meeting its goals? The best schools set the expectations and then follow through to meet those expectations.

5. Good Collaboration and Communication

Good schools are skilled at communicating and collaborating, both internally and externally. When teachers and administrators communicate well, it tells you a lot about the ethos of the school. It usually says that the school has an open and cooperative culture in which people enjoy their work and encourage each other to do their best. Like any organization, a school whose staff like coming to work every day is probably a healthy and robust learning environment. A school that does an excellent job of collaboration is able to involve parents, community leaders, and outside organizations.

Collaboration with parents is vitally important. Many schools have gotten so burned by nagging, meddlesome, interfering parents that they have tried to keep them at arm's length. You can't blame a school for adopting this posture, but the better schools continue to extend an open hand to parents who want to volunteer or desire to get information about the academic progress of their children.

Collaboration with outside professionals is also an important issue to consider, especially if your child has any special needs that might affect his education. I know that some schools are great collaborators, but others clearly send a message that outside professionals are an unwanted intrusion. Within recent months, I started seeing an extremely bright kid with some serious attention problems that interfered with his schoolwork. He went to one of the most competitive, academically challenging private schools in town, which had a long waiting list of kids. Nonetheless, every one of this boy's teachers and his guidance counselor agreed to meet with me to work on a plan to help him salvage his struggling year. After the meeting, I got weekly progress reports through the end of the school year to help me know how things were going. Not surprisingly, this boy, who was in danger of failing the grade, pulled through. For kids like him, the school's willingness to collaborate and communicate with outside professionals is vital.

Aslo the best schools also collaborate with outside agencies and organizations. This serves as good public relations for the school and it also gives the school greater access to services and resources. Several schools have entire buildings or stadiums paid for by a corporation. This wouldn't be possible without good collaboration. And schools with good relationships with other agencies can refer their students to the right services to help them get what they need. Communication and collaboration are an essential part of being a good school.

6. Monitoring of Teaching and Learning

The best schools know what is being taught and can assess what is being learned. Although teachers are free to set their own lesson plans and come up with innovative ways to teach, there is accountability around the presentation of content and around whether the students are learning it. Also, in recent years, there has been more focus on end-of-grade testing. This has been met with the criticism that this promotes only "teaching to the test" rather than teaching to help a child learn or grow to love learning. The criticism has some merit, but, overall, the monitoring of teaching and learning is still a good practice.

7. Professional Development

For some schools, teacher workdays are just a time to get caught up on grading or lesson plans. For anyone who has ever taught, this can be invaluable time. However, some of the better schools not only provide their teachers with adequate breaks to get their heads above water, but also have a full calendar of ongoing training and professional development.

Having done many of these trainings for teachers, school counselors, school psychologists, and administrators, I can tell you that you can read the culture of a school by the attitudes of the staff who show up for training. Schools that have a culture of excellence nearly always have staff who are intellectually curious and want to learn more. In contrast, the underperforming schools have overwhelmed staff who feel like it is a burden to go to a half-day of training. The best schools not only provide ongoing professional development and training, but also create a culture that values getting better and learning more.

* * *

School is a central part of a child's life. If your child goes to an excellent school, is a good reader, is bonded to his school, and is a good overall student, then count four protective factors in his favor. If he's lacking one or two, then the good news is that nearly all of these things can be added or enhanced. Remember, in your quest to get your child the best educational experience, don't be one of those parents who drive schools and teachers crazy. You can advocate for your child, but don't do it in an adversarial way if at all possible. While you're at it, also remember not to be one of those parents who drive their kids crazy. Better to preserve the relationship whenever you can.

10

Personality Protective Factors

Have you ever said that someone has a "good personality?" What exactly did you mean by that? It's one of those things that you sort of know intuitively but might be at a loss to define. Most psychologists agree that personality refers to the unique combination of attitudes, interests, and behavioral and emotional traits that seem to endure over a long period of time. One psychologist defined it for me as "a set of patterns of relating to the world."

Over the years, there have been many attempts to measure personality. Decades ago, one psychologist proposed an idea that different body types were predisposed to certain personality traits. Rounder people were more likely to be jolly and gregarious, for example. Although these kinds of simplistic explanations are most certainly out of vogue, there continues to be a lot of interest in studying and measuring personality.

In recent years, some researchers have taken the information from multiple personality tests, put them into a big statistical stew, and determined that there are five clusters of personality traits that seem to consistently emerge from all the data. They've come up with a few tests that, in the tradition of good psychological testing, have obscure initials, such as the NEO-PI, the BFI, the TDA, and others. You don't need to know the tests as much as you need to know what they measure. The Big Five, as these traits are now called, are

- *Conscientiousness*—the pattern of being responsible, dependable, and orderly
- *Openness*—the trait of being an independent, divergent, and imaginative thinker
- *Extraversion*—the tendency to be social, outgoing, talkative, and to positively assert
- *Agreeableness*—the quality of being cooperative, trusting, and easy-going
- *Neuroticism*—the inclination to experience frequent negative and upsetting emotions

People who score highly on these traits usually react a certain way in certain situations. For example, a person who scores highly in conscientiousness will likely be responsible at home, at school, and in the community. Another person who rates highly in openness will tend to approach most situations with a broad mind and a willingness to consider new thoughts. Different combinations of traits can yield different responses, so not all people who rate highly in extraversion will love going to parties, for example. However, there are some consistent findings about the various traits. Most of these results are exactly what you would expect. Here are some examples:

- Highly conscientious children tend to get better grades and grow up to become teenagers and adults who are good workers.
- Individuals who rate highly in conscientiousness usually have better health and live longer.
- Highly open children tend to be good overall students and are often more creative.
- Highly open people are much more comfortable with complexity and ambiguity.
- Highly extraverted children and teenagers are often more popular (especially if they are not high in neuroticism) and tend to be leaders in their schools and among their peers.
- People high in extraversion get less anxious when they are given constructive feedback.
- People who are more agreeable tend to be more charitable.
- Children who rate low on agreeableness and conscientiousness are more prone to delinquent and antisocial behavior.
- People who are low on agreeableness or high on neuroticism usually are in worse health.
- Those scoring high on neuroticism have higher rates of anxiety and depression.

So when you talk about someone's personality, you are probably referring to his or her unique combination of conscientiousness, openness, extraversion, agreeableness, and neuroticism. The three personality protective factors that we found can be understood within the context of the Big Five. The first protective factor, having a likeable personality, is associated with high degrees of agreeableness and extraversion. The second factor, having a good sense of humor, is connected to high levels of openness. The final factor, good coping with stress, is affiliated with low levels of neuroticism and high levels of conscientiousness.

❑ Has a Likeable Personality

I went to a school meeting at a private school that was notorious for its rigidity. Their motto seemed to be "Do it our way or leave." I went there to advocate for a girl named Annie who had failed a few classes the previous semester and was now on academic probation and in danger of being kicked out at the end of the year. I knew that Annie had a learning disability in reading that made a lot of her schoolwork difficult for her. I was prepared to push hard to get these teachers and administrators to be a little more flexible with her. However, as I went around the table and asked them about where we stood, a common theme emerged.

"I really like her," said the first teacher, "and I think she can do well here."

"Yes, she's such an enjoyable student," said the next. "I think she'll do fine if she can stay on top of her assignments."

"She's a terrific person," said the third.

This sentiment was echoed by nearly everyone around the table. This school, whose distinguishing feature was its adherence to strict academic standards, was telling me that they were going to work with her, cut her some breaks, and wanted her to stay. I'd had other interactions with the same school over the years and I got a lot of resistance. With Annie, I got none. Why? They liked her. It was as simple as that.

Having a likeable personality is probably the most intangible and hard-to-define protective factor. It's one of those "you know it when you see it" traits. However, there are some consistent characteristics of well-liked people. They usually have good social skills. They treat other people with respect and are helpful when someone is in need. They are more comfortable in new social situations and they have greater overall emotional intelligence. Basically, they are nice people who do nice things.

Some researchers have classified children into five groups based on how they are perceived socially: popular kids, average kids, rejected kids, neglected kids, and controversial kids.

Popular Kids

Although popularity and likeability are not identical concepts, they are closely related. Popular children tend to be likeable and likeable children tend to be popular. The truly popular children are liked by many peers and disliked by few peers. Although it is true that popular kids are often better looking, taller, and more athletic, most of the variables that determine popularity have to do with personality qualities. As you look over the list of characteristics of popular children, you will notice several of the protective factors described in this book. This isn't necessarily an exhaustive list, but here are twenty characteristics that various studies in child development found to be true of the popular kids:

1. They have good social skills.
2. They show greater empathy.
3. They have a good sense of humor.
4. They have good social problem–solving skills.
5. They have a secure attachment to parents.
6. They show confidence in new situations.
7. They have easier temperaments.
8. They are helpful to peers.
9. They engage in more cooperative play with peers.
10. They have good emotional awareness.
11. They are not overly reliant on others.
12. They easily adapt to new social situations.
13. They tend to maintain a positive tone in their peer relationships.
14. They initiate interactions in social situations.
15. They tend to be more assertive (sticking up for self) without being aggressive.
16. They are less verbally and physically aggressive.
17. They pick up more subtle social cues.
18. They accurately read the intentions of others.
19. They regulate their emotions well.
20. They actively avoid other children who provoke them.

Average Kids

Truly popular children are usually well liked or at least well regarded by their peers. In contrast, average children tend to get mixed reviews from their peers. Overall, they get along fine, though sometimes they may have a more harsh or verbally aggressive style than the more popular kids. The average kids are not the ones who get overlooked; they are just the ones who run in the middle of the pack.

Rejected Kids

Rejected kids seem to come in two varieties. The first type are the kids who are rejected because they tend to be more verbally and physically aggressive than their peers. Frankly, other kids don't want to play with them or even hang out with them because of their negative behavior. Aggression is the single leading cause of peer rejection. These aggressive rejected children tend to lack good social skills, but at the same time they overestimate their social abilities. They think they get along just fine, so they don't tend to evaluate their behavior or modify it much. They see other kids as being meaner and more malicious than actually intended, so they have an almost endless well of conflict. When there is a disagreement, these aggressive rejected kids have a hard time coming up with constructive solutions like taking turns or sharing, so they perpetuate more hostility. Overall, these children have tremendous difficulty in their social relationships and are typically the least liked among their peers.

One type of aggressive rejected child is the bully. Although there are some popular bullies, our research points to the fact that most bullies are extremely unpopular children. Bullies can come from both functional and dysfunctional families, but their parents often have common characteristics. They frequently have negative emotional attitudes toward the child that get communicated directly and indirectly. These adults frequently lack warmth and aren't regularly involved with their children. They also use a lot of power-assertive ("you'll do it right now!") methods of parenting and often resort to use of physical punishment. Despite this, they often have a dismissive attitude toward childhood aggression. They are of the "boys will be boys" mentality to an extreme. Often these are the parents who vigorously defend their child's misbehavior and cast lots of blame during school meetings, but then go home and beat the tar out of their kid. In general, it's not hard to figure out where the bullying attitudes got their start.

The other type of rejected kid is the withdrawn child who does not engage socially with peers. These children have less confidence in their own social abilities and they are much more likely to feel nervous around their peers. About 10–20 percent of rejected kids are the withdrawn type. They don't cause anyone much trouble, but no one really likes them, either.

Neglected Kids

A fourth group of kids are the neglected children. These are children who are neither liked nor disliked. They are sort of invisible to the other kids. Although they may be slightly more aggressive or disruptive than their peers, they tend to do it at such a low or infrequent level that they don't call much attention to themselves. They are the kids who don't get invited to sleepovers or birthday parties. In larger classes, they are some-times the children who aren't even known by name.

Controversial Kids

Finally, there are the controversial children. These are the kids who are actively disliked by some peers and loved by others. They often have an interesting combination of characteristics—often acting aggressive and disruptive, but also being humorous and cooperative. Some of them have a specialty niche, such as sports, art, or music. Others just have a distinc-tive look and sense of fashion. Some view them as arrogant and snobby, but others see them as friendly and supportive. They polarize people. You either love them or you hate them.

* * *

As a parent, your goal shouldn't be for your child to be popular. Your goal should be to help her be more likeable. There are some parenting approaches that can affect her likeability, and subsequently her popularity. Children rated highly on both likeability and popularity tend to have

- Mothers who are socially confident
- Mothers with good verbal skills
- Mothers who are both warm and firm
- Mothers who have more prosocial attitudes
- Fathers who are more physically playful
- Fathers who are more affectionate
- Fathers who are more socially engaging
- Parents who teach social skills
- Parents who provide frequent opportunity for peer interaction

In contrast, the parents of less socially competent, less popular, and less likeable children tend to use lots of harsh discipline and often respond to their children in overly controlling and authoritarian ways. They also hold a belief that their child's nature is predetermined and cannot change. They think that the child was just "born that way," so it follows that they don't do much to teach new skills or model prosocial attitudes and behaviors.

If you want to promote greater likeability in your child, I have a few specific steps you should consider:

- Teach and practice good social skills
- Model good ways to interact with others

- Give them opportunities to be helpful to others
- Help them develop some unique skills that will attract others
- Emphasize the importance of a good smile and eye contact

❑ Has a Good Sense of Humor

Over the years, I have known some funny kids, but none has been as hilarious as Malcolm. He was a teenage boy who struggled with depression, but he was possessed of the most slashing, spontaneous wit. Once he told me about crashing into a pickle truck on his bike and it made me laugh so hard the other psychologists down the hall asked me afterward, "What was *that* all about?" There were many times that Malcolm would get me going so much I'd have tears streaming down my face and my stomach hurt. He could take the most routine event—visiting a friend in a college dorm room or walking through the rain—and make it a stand-up routine that rivaled Jerry Seinfeld or, more similarly, Chris Rock.

Malcolm's sense of humor was a clear protective factor for him. It made him exceedingly likeable and it was a great way for him to cope with some of the difficulties in his life. Despite a lot of family nonsense and his own depression, he was able to do really well. He ended up going to college and making some close friends, and he continues to move forward in life, his sense of humor leading the way.

For many kids like Malcolm, having a good sense of humor is a protective factor for a number of reasons. It's fascinating to study the benefits of humor because you realize that it actually can strengthen other protective factors. Humor helps build new cognitive skills, it can increase vocabulary and knowledge of word meanings, it improves early reading skills, and it can increase creativity. Emotionally, kids who have a good sense of humor have more joy and happiness, they feel better about themselves, and they have another skill to cope with stress. When we laugh really hard, our brain produces endorphins—those little chemicals that make us feel better.

Dr. Paul McGhee is one of the leading researchers on how children develop humor. After a couple of decades of studying how their humor evolves, he has been able to identify some clear progressions and stages. His research is really helpful for parents with younger kids and truly intriguing for the rest of us, so I want to share some of his work with you, along with some other observations about kids and humor.

For the first six months of life, children laugh—often laughing a lot—but it has nothing to do with humor. Typically, they laugh at anything that arouses them, such as being thrown up in the air and caught or being tickled.

Between six months and the end of the first year of life, children learn to laugh at their parents—a trend that will continue in different forms throughout one's life! Infants love it when their parents make funny faces or moo like a cow. Imitating noises will also get big laughs out of these little ones. Infants see these things as funny because they recognize that they are different from how things are normally. Cows moo, not daddies.

After this stage, kids who are one to three years old are amused when anyone treats an object like it is a different object. Wearing a stuffed animal on your head like a hat or answering your shoe when the phone rings is guaranteed hilarity. Around three years old, children love to misname objects or actions. Humor is built on something being wrong or the opposite of how it is supposed to be. When one of my daughters was a preschooler, she used to be fond of saying, "Daddy is a mommy; mommy is a daddy." Children at this age begin to play with word sounds, though they aren't interested in the actual meaning. They'll just say nonsense words or words that rhyme over and over again, provoking near-nervous breakdowns in some parents. They also get a big kick out of combining words that don't fit together. When your son tells you that he wants a "hamburger bug," he's trying to be funny; he's not psychotic—unless he's 20 years old; then maybe you've got trouble.

Children who are three to five years old love to distort the features of things. They might do this in their drawings by adding things that don't belong (a person with wheels for feet) or changing the appearance of things (a square-headed person, an upside-down face) or making creatures do things that they wouldn't do (a dog wearing a suit, a cow flying). Perhaps Gary Larson of *Far Side* fame simply learned how to unleash his inner preschooler.

Kids who are four or five don't have a refined sense of humor, to be sure. They think accidents where someone falls down are a laugh riot. Gross things are hysterical, too. Poo-poo and booger humor can't be beat when you are a preschooler. (This trend continues well into adulthood, particularly for certain males.) By the time children are five, their humor focuses on such things as silly songs with silly movements and silly characters. Children in the first years of elementary school typically don't get jokes or riddles, but they love to give them a try.

She'll say something like "Knock, knock."

You answer, "Who's there?"

She says, "Cat."

"Cat who?"

"Cat food!" she screams and erupts in laughter.

She gets the setup and structure of the joke, but has no concept of where the humor is found. Around the age of seven, some cool things happen, though. As the child develops cognitively, humor begins to take some leaps forward. He can begin to understand riddles and puns. Verbal humor begins to take shape, especially with practice.

Some kids, like my boy Malcolm, are naturally skilled at humor. Their minds go to that absurd place, seeing contradictions, connections, and comparisons that other people don't see. They find funny things in observing everyday life or else they are wildly inventive in creating new realities.

Even if a child isn't especially skilled at humor, you can help her sharpen these skills in a lot of different ways. With younger kids, it's good to keep funny books around the house, sing funny songs together, put on skits, and model how to laugh at minor mishaps. Younger children are usually so naturally joyful and full of fun that good parenting is often simply not being a killjoy or a stick in the mud when they are being silly. It's good to show your kids that you think they are joyful and delightful whenever you can.

With older kids, sharpen up those skills by practicing riddles and puns. You can teach the process of constructing a joke. For example, you start with a simple object like a hot dog. Then you work backward. What else could this be? How about a real dog that is hot? How can we word that? Well, name a kind of dog. A poodle! Okay, what's another word for hot? How about "spicy"? Good one. A spicy poodle? Nah, let's make it a little bit better. What's a word that means "spicy" but also starts with a "p"? Tough one. Let's go with peppery. A peppery poodle. That's sounds great! Let's put it all together. What do you call a peppery poodle? A hot dog!

Now I doubt that you'll get that one on Leno, but you are less interested in how hysterically funny it is and more interested in teaching a way to think about humor, a way to construct setups and punch lines, and a way to think about being clever with words. It's also good to have some funny movies and shows that you watch together as a family. Modeling a sense of humor and celebrating funny things is as important as teaching a child how to create jokes. You may end up raising the next Ray Romano or Tina Fey—or maybe just a really funny kid who can count a good sense of humor among her protective factors.

❑   Has a Strong Ability to Cope with Stress

Over the years, I've had clients who have come to see me because they had a hard time coping with stress. There was the boy who threw himself down the stairs, the teenager who sat rocking back and forth in the dark while holding a butcher knife, and the girl who curled up in the fetal position on the back seat of the school bus, among dozens of others.

There's no evidence that this generation copes worse with stress than previous generations, but there is plenty of reason to believe that they are under more stress than in the recent past. Objectively, children and teens have more demands on them than ever before. Certainly they don't have some of the stressors of Depression-era kids or those who grew up during other times of hardship, but this generation faces more academic pressure—more kids are competing for the same number of college slots, there is more testing and accountability, and they report much more homework than previous generations—as well as family stresses that come from a strained economy. They are also growing up in a time of terror alerts and Amber alerts. The world feels scarier to adults, so you know it's got to feel unsafe to many children.

Stress can come from a lot of different things in a person's life, but three factors seem to be the most significant. The first is that stress seems to come from *change*. Did you ever see the old stress scale that was supposed to tally up all the stress points you have? If you recall, most of the stressors on there had to do with change—change in relationship status, change in your employment situation, change in home life, and so on. When things change, whether it is for good or bad, stress increases. For kids, this might be going from elementary school to middle school. That's a big stressor. Moving to a new neighborhood is a biggie. Having a friend move away can be a killer. All of these things are stressors, some of them good (grade promotion), some of them bad (friend leaving), and some of them neutral (a new neighborhood). Whether there are big stressors in your child's life or lots of little stressors all at once, make sure you tune into your child. Does she seem more irritable or withdrawn? Is he having more trouble concentrating or organizing himself? If so, it may have to do with stress.

A second factor that produces a lot of stress is *incompletion*. People seem to feel more stressed when there are lots of unfinished things in their lives. I hear this a lot from stay-at-home parents who feel like there is never an endpoint to their days or weeks. Laundry always accumulates, meals have to be cooked, and dishes are always piling up. Things never seem settled and completed. No wonder so many parents feel more stress when they stay at home with their children than when they have a full-time office job where there are clearly defined, manageable tasks.

Children seem to have the same experience. The more things they have hanging over their head in a state of incompletion, the more stressed they feel. As children get older and they have multiple school assignments at the same time, they are often going to feel more stress. When they've got too many projects or tasks going on at once, you should expect their level of stress to increase.

A third big source of stress is *anxiety*. We live in an anxious post-9/11 world that prepares students for school lockdowns and backpack searches. Though the reality is that kids are safer in their school than in their own home or neighborhood, many kids and their parents are terrified of having another Columbine or worse. On a more daily basis, older students are worried about doing well academically and getting into a decent college. This is no exaggeration: I recently had a high school senior with a 4.0 and a 1410 on his SATs ask me whether he had a decent chance of getting into a state school. It was no surprise that his parents had filled his head with horror stories of national merit scholars who didn't get into the same school. As we discussed in a previous chapter, we have a lot of nervous, worried parents among us. That translates to many anxious, stressed-out kids.

How can you help your child increase her ability to cope with stress? There are a lot of really practical things that you can do to help build these skills. Begin by teaching your child how to anticipate stressors. Explain the concept of stress and what causes people to feel stress. See whether she can generate a list of things that might cause her to feel stress. From there, you want to discuss how stress affects people emotionally, mentally, and physically. Help her recognize these effects and be aware when they start to happen. For example, if she begins to have trouble sleeping or to feel more irritable, you want her to connect the dots, seeing the relationship between stress and these difficulties. Finally, you want to teach her some simple strategies for coping with stress. Here are just a few examples:

- *Relaxation*—Picture a relaxing scene with your eyes closed; take slow deep breaths; relax all your muscles, starting with your feet and going up step by step to your head and face.
- *Stress cards*—Take notecards and write down everything that feels stressful at the moment; put them in order from most stressful to least;

then put them in categories of "Things I can control" and "Things I can't control." Tear them up and throw them away.

- *Journaling*—Write down thoughts and feelings in a diary or journal; many older kids have started doing this online.
- *Exercise*—Lots of kids use physical activity and exercise as a way of destressing; when you break a sweat and have all those endorphins swimming in your head, it's hard to feel as stressed.
- *Talking*—Practice talking about feelings and stressors with friends or family members; this is one of the best skills that you can develop to cope with stress.

It's also a good idea to help your child see the connection between good physical health and stress management. Eating healthy foods, eliminating caffeine and refined sugars, and getting enough sleep every night are essential to coping well with stress. When kids aren't coping well, it's a good practice to review their lifestyle habits to see whether anything needs to be adjusted.

In my therapy work with kids, I often have them create a list called "Good coping" and another one called "Bad coping." The good coping list should include things like those discussed above, as well as other things such as listening to music, playing video games (in moderation), taking a warm bath, watching something funny, and so on. Depending on the kid's age, the bad coping list includes things such as anger outbursts, drinking, looking at pornography, compulsive spending, staying up too late, and many others. The goal is to get children to recognize that everyone copes with stress, but some do it in bad ways and others handle it in healthy ways. As they become more aware of this, they can begin to visualize that list of good coping skills and pick one that will really work for them in the moment. I often tell my clients that increasing the good coping skills is like adding tools to a toolbox. The more tools you have, the more things you can fix.

A final way you can help your kids manage stress is to show them how to move things from incomplete to complete as effectively as possible. Often this means that you have to list out everything you have to do and prioritize. Prioritizing lets you see what things must get done now, can get done later, and would be nice to do but may never get done. Think about your own life and my guess is that there are certain things at work and home that must get done pronto; there are lots of other things that you simply can't blow off, but they can wait; there are probably many other things that you'd love to finish—reading that stack of books, refinishing that piece of furniture, learning a new skill—but may never get done. The ability to prioritize and then to act purposefully and efficiently is a skill that can often be developed at an early age. The people who are able to do this well have a much greater sense of completion in their lives. Consequently, they tend to have far less stress.

* * *

If your child is likeable and funny with a good ability to cope with stress, you can credit her with three protective factors. If she is lacking in any of these areas, the good news is that all of them can be improved. Even better news is that these are really *fun* things to work on with your kids.

11

Social Protective Factors

Every October, I go on an annual fishing trip with my friend Todd and some other buddies. I've gone on this trip for about fifteen years in a row. Here's my little secret that I'm sort of embarrassed to share with you: I've never once gone fishing during these fishing trips. I've gone out on the beach with them, but I've never actually baited a hook. I grew up within walking distance of the Chesapeake Bay, so I've had my fair share of fishing experiences as a child, including one with my grandfather who somehow convinced me that I caught twenty-one catfish in a row. (I think it was the same fish each time, but I'm not really sure.) But as I got older, it just didn't appeal to me that much. I'd much rather sleep in and stay dry than get up early and wade into the cold Atlantic Ocean.

Why go on the fishing trip every year? Well, because it gives me a chance to rest, sleep in, play video games, watch movies, and eat fish. But those aren't the biggest reasons. The real reason I go is because my friendship with Todd is worth taking the time off from work and driving five hours to the beach. He's been a great friend for nearly two decades and I want to hang out with him.

Every year of our married life Ellen and I have vacationed with a group of friends that Ellen knew from her time at North Carolina State. Those friends, their spouses, and their kids now get together at Guy and Marie's vacation house every year. With five couples and thirteen kids between us, it's cozy, even in a big house, but it's one of the highlights of the year. One couple drives from Ohio; another from South Carolina; still another flies in from California. The kids, who range from college age to kindergarten, hang out with the others who are closest in age and run wild most of the time. The adults talk, play games, and go sightseeing. It's an amazing experience to have lifelong friends like these and to watch each other's kids grow up.

For the past dozen years, Ellen and I have also gotten together with three other couples every Sunday night to "walk through life together." We spend time talking about our marriages, our jobs, our kids, and other important aspects of our lives. We've made a commitment to do this until we are all old and senile (which for some of us is coming sooner than we had hoped!). It's become a priority for all of us.

I share all this with you to tell you that friendships are a vital part of my life. I like having friends I've known for decades and I will continue to know for decades to come. They are part of who I am. This is the power of relationships. I love being married to a great woman and having fun kids, but I also cherish my other friendships. For kids, family relationships are vitally important, but friendships are essential. Here are four social protective factors that can help your children thrive.

❑ Has Good Social Skills

Jessica returned from a leadership conference for middle school students with a big smile on her face. Her parents said they hadn't seen her this happy in months. "All the people there were so *nice*," she said. She showed her parents a sheet of paper filled with names, e-mail addresses, and phone numbers. In the three days she had been there, she had made more connections with these kids than she had in eight months at her school. The first evening back home, she was already online instant messaging one of her friends. Jessica, who had always been a smart and capable kid, had never been the most outgoing or socially competent girl. She was pleasant and kind, but she didn't take much initiative with her peers. As a result, she felt disconnected and alone.

Going to the weekend conference was a bit of a fluke. Her vice-principal nominated Jessica because she was the class treasurer, but not because she had been an especially good leader. He just thought it would be good for her to go. What she experienced at the conference was the power of social skills. Nearly all the kids there were outgoing and confident. They weren't necessarily the best students in school, though most of them did well academically. Instead, they were people who used their ability to navigate socially to help them exert influence on their peers. Within a matter of hours, they had made a connection with this girl who had struggled socially for months.

Some people are innately good with social skills in the same way some people are naturally gifted athletes or musicians. However, social skills can also be learned and practiced with great success. There are numerous business seminars and workshops that help managers, sales people, and administrators improve their people skills. There are also many "how-to" books written for adults who want to be successful in business or in life. My favorite of all these is the original self-help book, Dale Carnegie's *How to Win Friends and Influence People*, first published back in 1936. This is a brilliant book, but I would not have considered it for kids until

I visited a residential program in Asheville, NC. The program there was run by an excellent Harvard-trained psychiatrist named Kim Masters, who gave me a tour of the facility and, almost in passing, told me that he used Carnegie's book for their social skills training. I was intrigued and picked up a copy soon after that. To this day, I've not found a better text. Just consider his "Six Ways To Make People Like You":

1. Become genuinely interested in other people.
2. Smile.
3. Remember that a person's name is to that person the sweetest and most important sound in any language.
4. Be a good listener. Encourage others to talk about themselves.
5. Talk in terms of the other person's interests.
6. Make the other person feel important—and do it sincerely.

This is a formula that's pretty hard to beat. I often go over each of these six points with my clients and practice them over and over again. We talk about body language, active listening skills, ways to ask good open questions, and other skills all within this framework. Like any ability, getting good at people skills requires practice. Some people acquire these new skills quickly, whereas others take a long time to get the hang of it. I find it useful to start with the basic skills, give a homework assignment, then review how it went. If the basic skills go well, then we build from there.

Arnold Goldstein and his colleagues at Syracuse University produced a great book years ago called *Skillstreaming the Adolescent*, which was directed at teaching social skills to disruptive teenagers. What the book did well was break down each of fifty social skills into microsteps. For example, "Introducing Yourself" became (1) choose the right time and place to introduce yourself, (2) greet the other person and tell your name, (3) ask the other person his/her name if you need to, and (4) tell or ask the other person something to help start the conversation. What this book did was open people's eyes to the fact that seemingly basic social skills such as joining in a conversation or apologizing may have a series of little steps that some kids aren't aware of and don't know how to pull off without practice. Again, for some children, these skills are natural, but for others, they require some work.

You can teach good people skills in a way that doesn't feel unnatural or forced. It can be part of a regular routine that involves teaching the skills at home or in the car, then practicing them in public. For example, you might teach your younger child how to order at a restaurant and then go out to practice. For an older child, you might work on greeting new people with a firm handshake, a smile, and good eye contact before going to an open house at a new school.

Social skills also need to be modeled for kids. If a kid sees his parents using poor social skills, then he's got a pretty good chance of doing the same thing himself. Some parents may need to read Dale Carnegie's book or go to a workshop before they try to help their own children. For those of you who are socially skilled, make sure that your children get the chance to see you in action. Social skills can be both taught and caught.

❑ Has Friends Who Are Positive and Supportive

Lindsey had always been a good kid. Her grades were good, her behavior at home and school was excellent, and she was involved in lots of positive activities at school. All that changed in ninth grade. Suddenly, her grades dropped. She stopped going to club activities. She began lying to her parents about her whereabouts. She and a friend were caught shoplifting a watch at the mall. What went wrong?

In a word: Alicia.

Lindsey's parents can pinpoint almost to the day when she started to take a nosedive. It was the day she first went over her new friend Alicia's house. Since then, Lindsey's life has gone steadily downhill. However, the mere suggestion that Alicia might be a bad influence on her provokes a torrent of angry curse words and slamming doors.

For better or worse, peers have a powerful influence on kids. The older children get, the stronger the influence of peers becomes, peaking during the high school years. Negative peers cause trouble, but positive peers can bring lots of benefits. Many kids have blossomed socially and emotionally under the influence of healthy friends. When kids are younger, they naïvely follow after peers, but as kids get older, friends shape their core sense of identity. Close friends heavily influence the beliefs, values, and behaviors of preteens and teenagers.

Unfortunately some kids always seem to gravitate toward negative peers. If they switch schools to get away from negative influences, they seem to find the same type of kids at the new school. It is hard to connect these kids to positive friends. Despite your best efforts, they always seem to gravitate toward the fringe kids or the troublemakers. It's as if there is something in them that pulls them right toward those negative influences. In fact, that may be a good way to think about it. If your child persistently attaches himself to the wrong peers, you may want to consider that it isn't the situation, but his own personality or self-esteem issue. This might require you to focus more of your energy on how he sees himself and relates to others than on changing his situation.

Some parents are faced with a dilemma of what to do when their child is drawn to antisocial peers. They know these kids are a bad influence, but they also know that to restrict contact may lead to lots more conflict at home and possibly even greater sneakiness and deceit. It's admittedly a tough predicament and one to which there is no simple answer. To make the decision, I would weigh out several variables such as his temperament and personality and the seriousness of the concerns. For children who are easily led or persuaded, I would also tend to be more cautious, especially when they are younger. When there are serious concerns, especially around safety, I would also be more cautious and restrictive.

I've known many parents who didn't want their kids hanging out with certain peers, but when I pressed the issue, they just "had a feeling" about the other kids, didn't like their haircuts or music, or something else that wasn't by itself enough cause for concern to be overly restrictive. In general, it is not a good idea to micromanage your child's relationships. Usually this ends in failure or at least resentment. However, you have to do a cost-benefit analysis. If you have genuine concerns about safety, respect, or honesty, then I would step in; otherwise, I would let him make his own choices.

I've known many children and teenagers who don't have positive friends because they don't have easy access to them. The kids at school or in the neighborhood are either negative or rejecting and they aren't involved in sports, scouts, youth group, or things like that. For your child to get connected with healthy peers, you have to put him in the path of these kids. Join the YMCA or the Jewish Community Center or some similar organization. Get involved with a service organization. Get him on a sports team, in the chess club, or youth group. Do something to get him around these positive kids. If you look around and all you see is negative peer influences, it means you have to start looking elsewhere for a place where your child can make a connection with healthy peers.

❑   Gets Support from Members of the Same Religious Faith

One summer day, Paul showed up for his session holding a big guitar case. He asked whether he could leave it in my office while we did the testing. "It's too hot in my car," he explained, "and I really don't want my guitar to get messed up." I told him that would be fine, but out of curiosity I asked him why he had the instrument with him. He said he was going to practice after our appointment.

"Are you in a band?" I asked him.

"Sort of," he said, "It's a worship band for my youth group."

"How long have you been doing it?" I asked.

"Since ninth grade," the eleventh grader told me.

"You must really like it, then," I said.

"I love it," he said, "It's my favorite part of my whole week."

"Better than the weekend?" I asked.

"Oh yeah. Way better."

Millions of children and teenagers are involved in youth groups in their faith communities. For most of them, it is a decidedly good thing. The research consistently shows that kids who are involved in youth groups and have an active spiritual faith are more likely to do well in many aspects of life. Studies involving thousands of teenagers have found that the kids who were involved in worship services, reading the scriptures, and praying reported less alcohol and drug use, delays in the onset of sexual activity, and greater prosocial and altruistic behavior.

Even among high-risk youth, active participation in faith and a faith community is a protective factor. When researchers surveyed over 1,700 urban adolescents, they found that the ones who had witnessed the most violence but who had actively practiced their own faith reported fewer conduct problems over time. They also found that the children who had been victimized the most, either by seeing upsetting things or experiencing them directly, but considered themselves to be very active in their faith reported fewer conduct problems than their nonreligious peers.

Faith is important not just for kids but for entire families. Studies consistently support the notion that families who are involved in faith communities do better on a wide range of outcomes. Parents in these families report greater marital satisfaction than average, along with greater overall family satisfaction and better parent-child relationships. These families tend to see less domestic violence and are less abusive and harsh with their children than other families. One study found that children in families that attended a worship service at least once a week were more likely to have better relationships with both their mothers and fathers. The mothers in the study were better able to be warm and firm with their children than parents who didn't attend services, and they were more likely to know their children's friends and who their kids were hanging out with when they were not at home. The fathers were rated as more consistent and supportive and their children were more likely to say they wanted to be like their dads when they grew up.

One boy, a kid named Allan, told me, "My closest friends are in my youth group. Other kids in my school are always doing stupid stuff, but me and my friends can hang out and have just as much fun as the ones who are out getting drunk or stuff like that. We just enjoy doing other things like going to movies or playing basketball."

The Search Institute found that youths who were involved in communities of worship were more likely to have other protective factors (or "developmental assets" as they refer to them) than nonreligious youths. In fact, of the forty protective factors, youths who were active in their faith had a total of five more on average than those who were not active in their faith. Those children and teens who were involved in a faith community on a weekly basis were more likely to have thirty-nine of the forty developmental assets than their peers. The Search Institute found that these spiritually minded kids were especially more likely to show good self-control and to be of service to others on a regular basis.

The beauty of youth group involvement is that it seems to increase other protective factors, especially the social ones such as having good social skills, having positive and supportive peers, and allowing involvement in a positive group activity, like Paul's involvement in the worship band. If you are not involved in a faith community, it might be time to consider going.

❑   Is Involved in At Least One Positive Group Activity

Deion Branch was a tiny little kid who got cut from his middle school football team because he was too small. He says that his coach kicked him off the team bus because he was afraid that Deion would get hurt. But the resilient little kid persisted, pushing himself to be better and better. A little over a decade later, Deion was named the Most Valuable Player of the Super Bowl—all 5'9" of him.

What makes this story even more incredible is that before the big game, Deion reportedly called every coach in his life who had helped him along the way, from Pee Wee league to college, more than a dozen coaches in all. In his excellent *Sports Illustrated* article about Deion's Super Bowl day, Rick Reilly writes, "Super Bowl MVP Deion Branch understands that being a great athlete is the work of dozens of people, not one."

There is almost nothing that is as emotionally stirring as a great sports story. Those old enough to remember will never forget the 1980 U.S. Olympic hockey team's victory over the Russians. They love to recall coach Jim Valvano running out onto the floor to hug somebody— anybody—in NC State's upset victory of the heavily favored Houston team. They'll still talk about tiny Doug Flutie heaving a no-chance desperation bomb in the final six seconds of the game to put trailing Boston College over the top. These are moments that stay with us. Ellen and I love to watch the Olympics and enjoy those exhilarating moments when the hair on the back of your neck stands up. There is a power in sports to stir us, infuriate us, and inspire us like few other things. At its purest, there is almost a magical quality to it.

Not far from my house, there is a big YMCA with giant fields in front of it. On any Saturday when the weather is decent, there are literally hundreds of kids out there filling up the fields learning soccer or lacrosse or other sports. It's a good sight. It's one of those little things that make me hopeful about our children.

On my way to work, I pass a house adjacent to a church that serves as a scout headquarters. On many Friday afternoons, the parking lot is full of kids in their scout uniforms packing vans for a weekend trip. I'm grateful that scouting is still going strong. We still have girl scouts who come through our neighborhood selling those addictive thin mint cookies.

I have a client named William who always seemed to be out of step with his peers at school. He had a learning disability and he didn't have the best social skills in the world. However, he discovered he was a talented actor and began auditioning for plays. One evening after a rehearsal for *the School Musical,* he loudly announced that he was going to a certain restaurant for dinner and he wanted people to come along. More than forty members of the cast and crew answered the call, cramming themselves into the little eatery. He was beaming as he told me the story a few days later.

Sports, scouts, plays—just a few examples of positive group activities that are helpful to kids. Dr. Barrie Morganstein, a clinical psychologist who works with children and teens in her practice, says, "Involvement in group activities increases a child's opportunities for feelings of success and mastery which in turn increase that child's self-esteem." She's absolutely right. When a kid gets involved in some group that fits his passions and talents, he has the chance to experience success in a way that he never could without having been a part of it.

Though it makes good intuitive sense, have you ever wondered why things like sports and scouts and clubs are so good for children? How do these group activities help kids? Here are several reasons why this kind of involvement is beneficial:

- *They involve disciplined activity*—Nearly all these activities involve some level of formal or informal rules, whether it is a sport, scouts, or the school play. You have to follow certain social conventions and discipline your behavior accordingly.
- *They tend to attract more positive kids*—Most participants of group activities are generally prosocial individuals who want to be with other healthy peers. The more antisocial or asocial kids don't tend to gravitate much toward group activities. Kids who are involved in these groups tend to be socialized to other children who are motivated, positive, and want to play by the rules.
- *They teach important life skills*—Group activities teach a wide range of life skills, such as strategy, decision making, problem solving, and more specific abilities. If you were in a scout troop, a chess club, or on a sports team, think of the skills that you picked up from that experience.
- *They expose kids to positive adult role models*—Coaches, instructors, and other leaders can often be a big influence on children and teens. I know several parents who rely on these adults to reinforce certain messages or to talk with their children when they are having a difficult time. Many of these adults end up serving as long-term role models for some of these kids. Just ask Deion Branch.

Some children naturally gravitate toward these group activities. You can't keep them off the ball field or they like the scout uniforms or they want to play for the school jazz band. However, there are always the kids who don't want anything to do with these sorts of things. They want to stay home and play video games or instant message all night. These are the kids that you can't even bribe to go out for the soccer team. What should you do? Knowing this is a protective factor, should you force them to do it? What if they protest or even refuse; should you push it? These are tough questions that parents often confront.

In general, I'd say no, you shouldn't force your kid to go kicking and screaming to try out for the play. However, it really depends on the child and the culture of the family. I know several parents who have successfully created a family culture that says every child must be involved in at least one group activity during the school year. Each child is free to choose what that activity is going to be, but choose she must. I think that is wise and commendable, but I would weigh out the potential costs against the potential benefits of such a requirement.

It's worth mentioning that part-time work is not the same as extracurricular involvement. In fact, the research on part-time work in high school generally says that it has negative effects. It seems as though extracurricular activities promote strong identification with school and with the values that the school is promoting. In contrast, part-time employment appears to undermine those connections to the school and its values. When kids work during the summer or if they are working to save money for college, it doesn't seem to have the same negative effects, so the issue is *when* they work and *why* they work.

If you had to sum all this up, it would be safe to say that extracurricular involvement—but not part-time work during the school year—is good for kids. Ideally, it would be some activity that is affiliated with the school and promotes positive values such as perseverance, good sportsmanship, cooperation, and working toward a goal. As a parent, it's important to promote these activities, but I wouldn't push too hard if it ends up becoming a negative thing between you and your child. You don't want to trade one protective factor (warm relationship with parents) for another (extracurricular involvement). Most kids, though, need to get involved!

12

Family Protective Factors

Andrew's reputation at school was not good to say the least. Everyone knew him as the pot-smoking delinquent who skipped class in the morning and reappeared later in the afternoon to catch his ride home. Though he seemed to be intelligent, he rarely showed it. His conversation with school staff was just a series of grunts and angry stares. His shaved head did not help matters either. It just reinforced the fact that he was a thug. A few weeks ago, he was picked up for underage drinking and possession of drug paraphernalia.

Andrew's poor parents were among the sweetest people in the world. They were kind and patient, almost to a fault. They knew they had not set good limits on him in the past and now they had an even harder time doing it because they were scared of his explosive anger. They were still patching the holes he punched through the walls in his room when they tried to ground him. However, they knew something had to be done. He was imploding, and it was only a matter of time before something really bad happened.

I spent time with his parents trying to stiffen their spines so they could take the right action with him. We started developing a list of all the people who were significant in his life. The only friends whom he had were other druggies who either reinforced his behavior or didn't care enough about him to try to slow him down. He had long ago dropped out of youth group and he hadn't played an organized sport in at least five years. No one else connected with him besides family members.

When Andrew came home one Thursday evening, the living room was full of people—his parents, his older brother home from college, his grandparents, who had driven through two states, aunts and uncles, a few cousins, and a great-grandmother who was in her eighties. His first impulse was to turn around and leave because he knew what was coming. But for some reason, he came into the room and sat down. His grandparents and some others in the room had never heard him cuss or explode with anger, so he was sure to speak in a composed voice.

"What's going on?" he asked.

"Andrew," his favorite uncle began, "we're all here because we love you and we want to help you."

Thus began an old-fashioned intervention that went on for more than three hours. At times he raised his voice and got out of his chair as if to leave, but it never got out of control. Finally, at the end, his grandfather spoke.

"We care deeply about you," said the older man, "and we will not only give up one night to help you but we will give up everything we have to help you."

At this, the tough as nails boy with no friends and no future collapsed into sobs. He came undone because of his family's love for him.

The road after that was still bumpy in spots but he graduated from high school, took some classes at a community college, and got a steady job. More important, he remains close to his parents and the rest of his family and continues to spend time with them.

Families are powerful, and the good ones serve to protect children, even the tough kids. We found three specific protective factors related to family life that benefits kids: having an easy temperament (because this is seen primarily in a family context when the child is young), feeling a strong connection to family, and having a warm and positive relationship with parents.

❑   Had an Easy Temperament

"She's such an easy baby!"

How many times have you heard a parent claim something like that? If it's a first-time mom, she probably can't believe her good fortune and might even be wondering when the hard times are coming. If it's a more experienced mom, she's usually just grateful, knowing how tough infants can be. There is no mistaking the fact that some babies are easy and some are difficult.

We know that having a difficult temperament can predispose a person to a whole lot of difficulty in life, especially in such things as relationships and emotional stability. However, the reverse is also true. Children who have an especially easy temperament have a protective factor from birth.

Different studies have conceptualized different aspects of temperament; some say there are nine, others say five. Sometimes they call the same basic concepts different things. Nonetheless, there is a remarkable amount of agreement around what constitutes temperament. Here are the dimensions that most people tend to agree on:

- *Sociability*—Children with easy temperaments are friendlier and less socially inhibited. They are freer and more comfortable around strangers and in social situations.

- *Emotionality*—Kids with easy temperaments tend to be less emotionally intense in their reactions and don't show as much negative emotionality, such as anger or fear.
- *Flexibility*—Children who have easier temperaments are more likely to adapt to changes in their routines, schedules, and surroundings.
- *Activity*—Easy temperament usually means having a low or at least moderate activity level most of the time.
- *Persistence*—Kids with easy temperaments tend to have high positive persistence, which means that they keep working on good tasks, even when they are tough. In contrast, they also are more likely to have low negative persistence, which means that they will not keep pushing when they shouldn't.

As I've said earlier, you can't do much about temperament. You can't make your child have an easy temperament if she doesn't already have one. Even though this is true, there are still a few things that you can do to help. First, make sure that you adjust your style as necessary to make the best fit with your child's temperament. Because "goodness of fit" is so important, the burden is on you to accommodate your child's way of reacting to the world. For example, if your child is intensely emotional, you have to work hard not to respond with intense emotional reactions. Instead, you will probably need to work on being calmer but firmer in your responses. If your child is less flexible, then you'll have to work harder to let her know ahead of time about changes in routine or schedule. The more extreme your child's temperament, the more you may have to adjust to make it a good fit. I've read some parenting articles that encourage parents not to change their style to fit their children. I understand the basic intent, which is not to let the kid be the boss, but I disagree with the conclusion. If you have a kid with a tough temperament, you would be wise to adjust your approach as needed.

Another good action step you can take is to teach skills that help reduce intensity. If your child is extremely overactive, then work on stop-and-think skills. If he is emotionally reactive, then teach anger control skills. If she is less sociable, then you will want to practice social skills. None of these things will keep a temperamentally difficult child from being difficult, but you can reduce the impact of some of those behaviors.

If your child has an easy temperament, make sure that you make the most of it and encourage him to develop good social skills and even better emotional regulation skills. Teach him the value of hard work and persistence, then reward him when he demonstrates it.

You may be wondering why this protective factor shows up in the family section. Although it is a more internally based quality, it has tremendous impact on the family and the family can exert some considerable influence back. Because temperament involves early patterns of interacting with and reacting to the world, most of it involves parents and siblings. Temperamentally tough kids can affect an entire family, but the family can also help shape up the temperament. Use your influence well. Be strategic, persistent, and wise.

❏ Feels a Strong Connection to Family

When I was a kid, I lived in the cool house in the neighborhood. Mine was the one where all the neighborhood kids would hang out and play. When we got to be teenagers, it continued to be the cool house. Part of it was because we were the first family to have cable TV, the first family to have a VCR (boy, I'm feeling old), and the only house on the street to have a pool table. But more than that, it was because I had cool parents. I had the mom and dad whom the other kids wanted to hang around. My dad coached baseball and shot pool; my mom was outgoing and fun. Although many kids seemed embarrassed of their parents, I was glad that my friends liked mine. I liked them, too.

My brother and I were also close, even though we were more than four years apart in age. My friends liked him; his friends liked me. We would play army men and kick ball and build forts together. We enjoyed being together and he and I remain close friends. We were each the best man at the other's wedding.

I know firsthand the benefit of having a tightly bonded family. Even though I live almost three hundred miles away from the rest of them, we continue to stay connected. Having such a strong bond to my family has spared me a lot of the angst that some of my peers experience even to this day. More than that, it gave me many things that help out my relationships and my career as an adult: my sense of humor, empathy, and good judgment are just a few traits that have served me well.

In my professional practice, I try never to miss the importance of family bonding. Children who are more attached to their family tend to do better, regardless of the presenting problem, than other children who have no strong connection to family members or to the family as a whole. This connection usually means that they see family members as allies in their struggle, rather than the reason for their difficulties. For example, if I have two thirteen-year-olds who are battling depression, all things being equal, the one who maintains connection to his family and leans on them for support will tend to do better than the other kid who wants his family just to leave him alone.

The research consistently points to the benefit of family bonding in the lives of children. Kids who are more attached to their families have lower rates of drug use and antisocial activity. Children who are more bonded to their families also tend to hang out with peers who are more positive and are more likely to get involved in healthier group activities. The benefits of family bonding extend well beyond the family.

I've known parents who have yearned for their child to have a stronger connection with the family, but the kid simply will not do it. There are a number of reasons for this. Sometimes children are not connected to their families because they have difficult temperaments or because of certain negative experiences, such as high family conflict or divorce. Other times, kids have trouble staying bonded to their families if they are influenced by negative peers who have values that run counter to their family.

There are also times when a child doesn't keep a connection and it is largely one or both of the parents' responsibility. Recently, I had a dad tell me, "We don't have anything in common. I like to play golf and he doesn't. He likes to skateboard and I think that's stupid. I'm not going to go out there and watch him skateboard or take him to one of those skate-board parks." To which I replied, "Why not?" After he explained that this was a foolish waste of time, I challenged him that the responsibility for connecting with his son was more on him than on the boy. I've also known a few parents who have their own attachment or trust problems that negatively affect their relationships with their children. They seem to lack the ability to form a bond. Consequently, it's no big surprise that their children don't have a connection to them or the family.

There are some really good ways to promote better family bonding with your children. The best suggestion is that the parents as individuals and the family as a unit need to be *where the fun is*. I mean this honestly. Parents who are fun, self-assured, and flexible are attractive to kids—and their peers. My wife and I have set a goal of making our family experience so fun and rewarding that our children want to have their friends over and they want to have us around.

This does not mean that the parents try to act like kids, be falsely hip, or fail to set limits. In fact, the parents who do these things will often be annoying at best and harmful at worst. Some of my clients have told me about parents in their neighborhoods who let the kids smoke pot in the basement or in the shed out back. Others have told me about moms who dress provocatively when their son's teenage friends come over. In case you were wondering, these sorts of things are not examples of good parenting.

It is possible to be fun and to make family life a blast while still maintaining parental authority and good boundaries. On Fridays, we have game night at our house. Nearly every Saturday, I take my own kids out for something fun. It might be the IMAX theater or the park or the mall. We take vacations together. We take our fun seriously.

I know that it is harder to maintain this connection with teenagers than it is with younger kids, but the same process applies. It even works for surly adolescents! One of the best things you can do for your kids is to give them a fun childhood, because if they hit a tough stretch in those teenage years, they are more likely to rebound and land on their feet with the family. I continue to be impressed with the parents who have maintained heart connections with their children, even during the most difficult times. As a result, I've seen how much easier it is for their kids to come back emotionally once the dust has settled.

Many families have regular family meetings to increase cohesiveness and bonding. In these meetings, decisions about the daily life of the family are made, as well as planning for big events. The intent of these meetings is to make everyone feel important and valued in the family unit. They also allow any grievances to be aired and addressed in a direct and honest manner. These meetings model good communication, problem solving, and conflict resolution skills. It's a good practice for both younger and older children.

As kids get older, the influence of peers grows stronger, but it is still possible for a child to maintain a strong connection to his family. Don't believe the myth that says teenagers can't be close to their family. It may take more work, more flexibility, and more patience, but it can be done. Keep taking those family vacations and practice those family traditions. Keep working on it, even during the tough times.

❏   Has a Warm and Positive Relationship with Parents

There are many days at work when I see kids back to back who could not be more different from each other. One hour, I might have a reckless and fearless child who is jumping off the garage using an umbrella as a parachute; the next hour, I might see a kid who is so fearful he can't play in the yard without his parent sitting on the porch. I've seen a teenager who is smoking pot every day, and during the next session I have a kid who is so antidrug as to be militant about it. I have to switch gears so frequently during the day that I just take it for granted that this is part of the job. Nonetheless, I remember one day when I was floored by the contrast.

During the first hour, a fourteen-year-old boy named Jamie came in with his parents to talk about his problems with school. He hadn't been turning in his homework and he had been hiding his progress reports from his parents for fear that they would find out he wasn't doing well. Well, eventually, the cat was out of the bag and, by that time, Jamie was in danger of failing the quarter. His parents were frustrated and worried; Jamie was just discouraged and worn out by school. What struck me about the meeting was how sweet they all were with each other. His father would touch Jamie's shoulder as he spoke. His mother made it clear that they loved him very much. Jamie also said that he loved them, too, but he was just feeling buried and he didn't know what to do. As we all spoke, it was clear that we were all on the same page, working as a team of collaborators. By the end of an hour, we had a plan that seemed likely to work. It was basically a dig-out plan that involved more structure and accountability but also more rewards for working hard. After the session, the boy seemed visibly relieved and was physically playful with his dad as they stood up to go.

Ten minutes later, I'm sitting with another fourteen-year-old boy and his parents. This time, the boy, named Rick, sat down to talk about his failing grades. He hadn't been turning in his homework and he had been hiding his progress reports from his parents for fear that they would find out that he wasn't doing well. (Sound familiar?) His mother nearly immediately started to berate him.

"I can't stand your lying!" she said.

"I didn't lie," the boy protested.

"Yes, you did!" she shot back. "Every time you hid your progress reports or your assignment notebook from us you were lying."

Dad decided to jump in at this point. "You're just throwing your life away. Do you think that you will get into any college if you pull this kind of stuff next year in ninth grade?"

The boy sat there, his body slumped in the chair, his forearm over his eyes. He didn't respond. Both parents prodded him verbally.

"What do you have to say about this?" asked dad.

"What do you think we should do?" asked mom.

"Whatever," said the boy, not moving an inch.

I tried to plan something constructive, seeing whether we could all agree on some goals. What I realized was that both parents and the boy were there more to take shots at each other than they were to make it better. As soon as we'd get close to some kind of resolution or agreement, one of the parents would verbally lash the boy or the kid would tell them to shut up or some equally attractive response. Needless to say, the appointment was a bust.

Same problem. Same age kid. Same starting obstacles. Very different outcomes. The biggest variable, as far as I could see, wasn't the child's behavior or attitude; it was the relationship between the parents and the child. I can't overstate the importance of warm and positive relationships between kids and their parents. In situations like this, it makes all the difference in the world.

By the way, I don't put all the blame on Rick's parents. He was no prince himself. After a while, it became nearly impossible to figure out where it all started. Was it that the parents were unreasonable, pushy, demanding, never to be pleased that got the ball rolling? Or was it Rick's surly, dishonest, uncooperative attitude that got us here? My best guess is that it was both, an interactive effect between parents and child, a poor fit.

There are many children like Jerry and Rick. They are kids who don't live up to their potential or to parental expectations. Sometimes these kids have learning disabilities or attention problems; other times, they have problems with motivation for other reasons. Parents of these children often face a dilemma: push the achievement and lose the relationship or don't push them and face school failure. It's a hard place to be as a parent. On the one hand, you can ride herd on the child and he'll hate you but he might get better grades. On the other hand, you'll feel like you are shirking your parental responsibilities and dooming him to fewer options later in life. It's a tough decision. What are you to do?

Obviously, I can't tell you exactly what to do in a book because I don't know your unique child and your unique situation. However, I can tell you that it is a perfectly legitimate option to place relationship over achievement. In other words, it's okay to work on having a good connection with your child instead of having knockdown/drag-out battles over school effort and performance. You're not a bad parent if you choose a strong relationship over high achievement.

Here's my reasoning: If your child—especially once she gets into high school—is completely dependent on you to perform in school, then you are probably structuring her over her head. You are making her competitive for colleges that she might be able to get into but won't be able to maintain. In graduate school, I did an assistantship in the university counseling center. My job was to intercept the kids who were failing out of school and make a plan to help them stay in school. The profile was similar: smart kids with learning or motivation problems with strong parents who kept them on the rails throughout high school, only for the kids to get into a competitive college and then be out of their depth academically.

Another reason for not riding herd on these unmotivated or struggling kids is that it rarely works. I hardly ever see a big payoff for the amount of blood, sweat, and tears that parents put into these efforts. It's just not effective. These children often manage to thwart your best efforts, either intentionally or unintentionally. In the cost-benefit analysis, there is a lot of cost and little benefit.

A final reason for avoiding these big battles is that there are tremendous benefits to having a good connection with your kids. When the tornado of adolescence has passed by, you want them to land on their feet in their relationship with you. You might lose a protective factor (good overall student) but you'll at least gain or preserve another. What Rick's parents don't see is that they are ultimately choosing neither achievement nor relationship. He won't do better in school because they punish or berate him, and he certainly won't want to be with them when he moves into adulthood.

If your child is struggling in school and she invites you to help her, then by all means help her. However, if you find yourself in constant battle to get her to achieve, then it might be better to put your efforts toward liking and enjoying each other.

Whether your child has school struggles or not, the need for a warm and positive relationship with your child is a vitally important protective factor. You can't make your child like you, but you can at least try. Pardon me for stating the obvious, but you aren't likely to have a warm and positive relationship if you aren't warm and positive. Show interest in your child. Look him in the eye and really listen when he talks. Smile and laugh with him. Do silly things with younger kids and funny things with older kids (there is a slight but important difference for adolescents who are easily embarrassed by parental silliness). Be encouraging. Resist the urge to overlecture. Don't motivate by fear or anger. As much as you can, be fun, loving, and upbeat.

I know many parents who have tried to reach out to their children, only to have their hands bitten. It takes two to have a relationship and sometimes you can do your best and get nothing in return. I've talked to many parents who have known the heartache of being rejected by their kids. I encourage you to hang in there. Having done my job for enough years to see many tough kids repair their relationships with their parents when they hit young adulthood, I urge you to keep moving toward your children. There's no guarantee, but it's your best hope. You want to be able to say that you did your part and kept running after your kid even when he was pushing away from you.

For those of you who have good relationships with your children, don't take them for granted. Cherish them, nurture them, and work to preserve them. You have been blessed with something wonderful.

In the week that I was writing this chapter, I got an e-mail from a dad—a good man and father—telling me good news about his son. He and his wife had gone through nearly all the same things that Andrew's parents had experienced (the kid from the beginning of this chapter)—bouts of anger, barricading himself in the room, defiance, disrespect, drug use, expulsion, and more. He wanted to let me know that his son was going to graduate on time and go off to college. For this kid, this was quite an accomplishment. I'll let this dad have the last word for this chapter. He wrote, "Finally good news! . . . my wife and I will write a book someday on raising challenging kids! First lesson . . . never give up."

My Last Gasp

All of this really boils down to a simple message: if you increase the number of protective factors your child has, you will improve his chances of having a good life. Now that you know the protective factors and some practical ways to strengthen them, where do you start? Let me briefly give you three ways to take action.

FOCUS ON YOUR BEST BETS

There's no point in even trying to be a Supermom or Wonderdad who does it all. It simply can't be done. However, you might be able to focus on three to five protective factors that have the best chance of improving in your child. To help you decide, Table 1 gives the general chance of improving each of the protective factors.

	Chance of Improving			
Protective Factor	None	Low	Med	High
Easy temperament (easy-going, outgoing, curious)	X			
Has average or better intelligence	X			
Has a likeable personality		X		
Has friends who are positive and supportive			X	
Talks about feelings openly and honestly			X	
Cares about the feelings of others			X	
Feels bad after doing something wrong			X	
Has a good sense of humor			X	
Believes good choices lead to good resutls			X	
Is a good overal student			X	
Has strong interest is school			X	
Goes to an excellent school			X	
Feels a strong connection to family				X
Has a warm and positive relationship with parents				X
Has good social skills				X
Gets support from members of the same religious faith				X
Is involved in at least one positive group activity				X
Has a strong ability to cope with stress				X
Can come up with solutions to problems in life				X
Has positive and realistic goals for the future				X

Typically, such things as setting goals, learning problem-solving skills, and creating coping skills have the best chance of strengthening a protective factor. It's probably wise to focus on these areas, but you have to know your child. If your kid is strongly opposed to extracurricular involvement or can't tolerate the idea of setting goals right now, then I might not push those issues. I'd pick the areas where I had the best chance of having a solid impact. Focus on your best bets.

MAKE A PLAN

When you decide which protective factors to target, then your next step is to make a plan. Write out the specific protective factor(s), followed by the steps you will take to help build these into the life of your child. A plan for one of the protective factors might look something like this:

Goal: **To help Wes improve his social skills**
Steps: 1.   Teach him how to greet people well.
         2.   Teach him how to ask good open questions.
         3.   Practice eye contact with him in conversation.
         4.   Give him some practice opportunities with adults and other kids.

Now, if it isn't your style to be so fancy and formal, then don't feel like you have to write it out like this. As long as you have a strategy—either down on paper or just in your head—then you will likely get a good outcome. Make a plan.

BE PERSISTENT

One of the biggest errors that some parents make is that they throw in the towel too quickly. They hope their child will become more socially skilled or more attached to school or some other worthy goal, but they get disheartened when the kid doesn't grab hold of it quickly. Take note: some children learn certain skills or acquire new habits fairly quickly. Others take a while and require a lot of parental patience. Just hang in there and keep working at it. I promise you it's worth the struggle, so be persistent.

THE LAST WORD

Thanks for reading this book. I hope it has helped you gain confidence in both your parenting style and ability. The work you do from here on out will certainly be an investment in your child's future. Now, go love your kid!

References and Further Reading

1. Who Is This Millennial Generation?

Horatio Alger Institute (2003). *State of our nation's youth.* Alexandria, VA: Horatio Alger Association.

Howe, N. and Strauss, W. (2000). *Millennials rising: the next great generation.* New York: Vintage Original.

Smith, S. (2001). Should we be thankful for teens. Available at http://www.youthdevelopment.org/articles/op110106.htm.

2. A Whole New World

Barna, G. (2002). *Real teens: a contemporary snapshot of youth culture.* Ventura, CA: Regal Books.

Licinio, J. and Wong, M.-L. (2005). Depression, antidepressants and suicidality: a critical appraisal. *Nature Reviews Drug Discovery, 4* (2), 165–171.

Study: drugs prevent suicide (2005). *The Los Angeles Times,* February 4.

U.S. Food and Drug Administration (2004). FDA launches a multi-pronged strategy to strengthen safeguards for children treated with antidepressant medications. Press release, 15 October; available at http://www.fda.gov/bbs/topics/news/2004/NEW01124.html.

Vendantam, S. (2005). Antidepressants raise risk of suicide. *The Washington Post,* February 17.

Youth Violence Poll (1994). Gallup Poll Monthly, September.

3. What, Me Worry?

Collins, R., Elliott, M., Berry, S., Kanouse, D., Kunkel, D., Hunter, S., and Miu, A. (2004). Watching sex on television predicts adolescent initiation of sexual behavior. *Pediatrics, 114* (3), 280–289.

Kelly, K. and Kulman, L. (2004). Kid power. *U.S. News and World Report,* September 13, pp. 47–51.

Kluger, J. (2004). The kids are all right. *Time,* July 26, p. 53.

Quinn, Michelle (2004). Brat packs drive many parents to distraction. *Knight Ridder,* February 24.

RAND Corporation study, headed by Rebecca Collins (2004). Study links TV to teen sexual activity. Press release, September 7.

Sachs, A. (2004). Junk culture, an interview with Juliet Schor. *Time,* Bonus Section, October.

Schor, J. (2004). *Born to buy: the commercialized child and the new consumer culture.* New York: Scribner.

Tyre, P., Scelfo, J., and Kantrowitz, B. (2004). The power of no. *Newsweek*, September 13, pp. 42–51.

Woolf, A. and Lesperance, L. (2003). What should we worry about. *Newsweek*, September 22, p. 40.

4. Ten Traits of Good Parents

Baumrind, D. (1989). Rearing competent children. In W. Damon (Ed.), *Child development today and tomorrow* (pp. 349–378). San Francisco: Jossey-Bass.

Baumrind, D. (1991). The influence of parenting style on adolescent competence and substance use. *Journal of Early Adolescence, 11* (1), 56–95.

Covey, S. (1990). *The 7 habits of highly effective people: powerful lessons in personal change*. New York: Free Press.

Demo, D. and Acock, A. (1996). Family structure, family process, and adolescent well-being. *Journal of Research on Adolescence, 6*, 457–488.

Gaskill, F. (1997). A study of the relationship between memories of preadolescent family rituals and male adolescent behavior problems. Doctoral dissertation, University of North Carolina–Chapel Hill.

Maccoby, E. E. and Martin, J. A. (1983). Socialization in the context of the family: parent-child interaction. In P. H. Mussen (Ed.) and E. M. Hetherington (Vol. Ed.), *Handbook of child psychology*, Vol. 4. *Socialization, personality, and social development*, 4th edn. (pp. 1–101). New York: Wiley.

Quindlen, Anna (2005). The good enough mother. *Newsweek Magazine*, February 21, pp. 50–51.

Warner, Judith (2005). *Perfect madness*. New York: Riverhead Books.

Weiss, L. H. and Schwarz, J. C. (1996). The relationship between parenting types and older adolescents' personality, academic achievement, adjustment, and substance use. *Child Development, 67* (5), 2101–2114.

5. Kids with a Hope and a Future

Benson, P. L., Scales, P. C., Leffert, N., and Roehlkepartain, E. C. (1999). *A fragile foundation: the state of developmental assets among American youth*. Minneapolis: Search Institute.

Bernard, B. (2002). *The foundations of the resiliency framework: from research to practice*. San Francisco: Resiliency in Action.

Blyth, D. A. and Leffert, N. (1995). Communities as contexts for adolescent development: an empirical analysis. *Journal of Adolescent Research, 10* (1), 64–87.

Donahue, M. D. and Benson, P. L. (1995). Religion and the well-being of adolescents. *The Society for the Psychological Study of Social Issues, 51* (2), 145–160.

Maston, A. (1993). Resilience in individual development: successful adaptation despite risk and adversity. In M. Wang and E. Gordon (Eds.), *Educational resilience in inner-city youth*. San Francisco: Jossey-Bass.

Rutter, M. (1987). Psychosocial resilience and protective mechanisms. *American Journal of Orthopsychiatry, 57* (3), 316–331.

Sergiovanni, T. (1993). *Building community in schools*. San Francisco: Jossey-Bass.

Sharma, A. N., McGue, M., and Benson, P. L. (1996). The emotional and behavioral adjustment of United States adopted adolescents: Part II. Age of adoption. *Children and Youth Services Review, 18* (1/2), 101–114.

Vance, J. E., Bowen, B. K., Fernandez, G., and Thompson, S. (2002). Risk and protective factors as predictors of outcome in adolescents with psychiatric disorder and aggression. *Journal of American Academy of Child and Adolescent Psychiatry, 41* (1), 36–43.

Werner, E. E. (1989). High risk children in young adulthood: a longitudinal study from birth to 32 years. *American Journal of Orthopsychiatry, 59* (1), 72–81.

6.   Risk Factors

Costello, E., Keeler, G., and Angold, A. (2001). Poverty, race/ethnicity, and psychiatric disorder. *American Journal of Public Health, 91* (9), 1494–1498.

Gladwell, M. (2002). *The tipping point*. New York: Little, Brown.

7.   Emotional Protective Factors

Bar-On, R. and Parker, J. D. A. (Eds.) (2000). *The handbook of emotional intelligence: theory, development, assessment, and application at home, school and in the workplace*. San Francisco: Jossey-Bass.

Cherniss, C. (2000). Emotional intelligence: what it is and why it matters. Paper presented at the Annual Meeting of the Society for Industrial and Organizational Psychology, April 15; available at http://www.eiconsortium.org/research/what_is_emotional_intelligence.htm.

Eisenberg, N. and Fabes, R. A. (1991). Prosocial behavior and empathy: a multimethod, developmental perspective. In P. Clark (Ed.), *Review of personality and social psychology*, Vol. 2 (pp. 34–61). Newbury Park, CA: Sage.

Eisenberg, N., Fabes, R. A., Miller, P. A., Fultz, J., Mathy, R. M., Shell, R., and Reno, R. R. (1989). The relations of sympathy and personal distress to prosocial behavior: a multimethod study. *Journal of Personality and Social Psychology, 57* (1), 55–66.

Feist, G. J. and Barron, F. (1996). Emotional intelligence and academic intelligence in career and life success. Paper presented at the Annual Convention of the American Psychological Society, San Francisco, CA, June.

Goleman, D. (1995). *Emotional intelligence: why it matters more than IQ*. New York: Bantam.

Goleman, D. (1998). *Working with emotional intelligence*. New York: Bantam.

Gottman, J. (1997). *Raising an emotionally intelligent child*. New York: Simon & Schuster.

Kohlberg, L. (1981). *Essays on moral development: the philosophy of moral development*, Vol. 1. San Francisco, CA: Harper & Row.

Mayer, J. D., Caruso, D., and Salovey, P. (1999). Emotional intelligence meets traditional standards for an intelligence. *Intelligence, 27* (1), 267–298.

Mayer, J. D. and Salovey, P. (1993). The intelligence of emotional intelligence. *Intelligence, 17*, 433–442.

Mayer, J. D., Salovey, P., and Caruso, D. R. (2000). Models of emotional intelligence. In R. J. Sternberg (Ed.), *Handbook of intelligence* (pp. 396–420). Cambridge, U.K.: Cambridge University Press.

Meerum Terwogt, M., Koops, W., Oosterhoff, T., and Olthof, T. (1986). Development in processing of multiple emotional situations. *Journal of General Psychology, 113* (1), 109–119.

Merlevede, P. and Bridoux, D. (2001). *7 Steps to emotional intelligence*. Carmarthen, UK: Crown House.

Russell, J. A. and Ridgeway, D. (1983). Dimensions underlying children's emotion concepts. *Developmental Psychology, 19*, 795–804.

Salovey, P. and Mayer, J. D. (1990). Emotional intelligence. *Imagination, Cognition, and Personality, 9* (3), 185–211.

Schwartz, R. M. and Trabasso, T. (1984). Children's understanding of emotions. In C. E. Izard, J. Kagan, and R. B. Zajonc (Eds.), *Emotions, cognition, and behavior*. New York: Cambridge University Press.

Shoda, Y., Mischel, W., and Peake, P. K. (1990). Predicting adolescent cognitive and self-regulatory competencies from preschool delay of gratification: identifying diagnostic conditions. *Developmental Psychology, 26* (6), 978–986.

Snarey, J. R. and Vaillant, G. E. (1985). How lower and working class youth become middle class adults: the association between ego defense mechanisms and upward social mobility. *Child Development, 56* (4), 899–910.

Stein, N. L. and Jewett, J. L. (1986). A conceptual analysis of the meaning of negative emotions: implications for a theory of development. In C. E. Izard and P. Read (Eds.), *Measurement of emotion in infants and young children*. New York: Cambridge University Press.

Thorndike, R. L. and Stein, S. (1937). An evaluation of the attempts to measure social intelligence. *Psychological Bulletin, 34* (1), 275–284.

Wechsler, D. (1940). Nonintellective factors in general intelligence. *Psychological Bulletin, 37* (1), 444–445.

8.   Cognitive Protective Factors

Armstrong, T. (1993). *7 Kinds of smart: identifying and developing your many intelligences*. New York: Plume.

Basgall, J. A. and Snyder, C. R. (1988). Excuses in waiting: external locus of control and reactions to success-failure feedback. *Journal of Personality and Social Psychology, 54,* 656–662.

Bendell, D., Tollefson, N., and Fine, M. (1980). Interaction of locus of control orientation and the performance of learning disabled adolescents. *Journal of Learning Disabilities, 13* (1), 83–86.

Findley, M. J. and Cooper, H. M. (1983). Locus of control and academic achievement: a literature review. *Journal of Personality and Social Psychology, 44,* 419–427.

Gardner, H. (1993). *Multiple intelligences: the theory in practice.* New York: Basic Books.

Gibbs, N. (2005). Parents behaving badly. *Time,* February 21, pp. 40–49.

Gordon, D., Nowicki, S., Jr., and Wichern, F. (1981). Observed maternal and child behaviors in a dependency producing task as a function of children's locus of control orientation. *Merrill-Palmer Quarterly, 27,* 43–51.

Hans, T. (2000). A meta-analysis of the effects of adventure programming on locus of control. *Journal of Contemporary Psychotherapy, 30* (1), 33–60.

Hattie, J. A., Marsh, H. W., Neill, J. T., and Richards, G. E. (1997). Adventure education and outward bound: out-of-class experiences that have a lasting effect. *Review of Educational Research, 67,* 43–87.

Krampen, G. (1989). Perceived childrearing practices and the development of locus of control in early adolescence. *International Journal of Behavioral Development, 12* (2), 177–193.

Lepper, M., Greene, D., and Nisbett, R. (1973). Undermining children's intrinsic interest with extrinsic reward: a test of the "overjustification" hypothesis. *Journal of Personality and Social Psychology, 28* (1), 129–137.

Marsh, H. W. and Richards, G. E. (1986). The Rotter Locus of Control Scale: the comparison of alternative response formats and implications for reliability, validity and dimensionality. *Journal of Research in Personality, 20* (1), 509–558.

Marsh, H. W. and Richards, G. E. (1987). The multidimensionality of the Rotter I-E Scale and its higher order structure: an application of confirmatory factor analysis. *Multivariate Behavioral Research, 22* (1), 39–69.

Marshall, G. N. (1991). A multidimensional analysis of health locus of control beliefs: separating the wheat from the chaff? *Journal of Personality and Social Psychology, 61* (3), 483–491.

Miller, R., Brickman, P., and Bolen, D. (1975). Attribution versus persuasion as a means of modifying behavior. *Journal of Personality and Social Psychology, 31* (1), 430–441.

Paguio, L., Robinson, B., Skeen, P., and Deal, J. (1987). Relationship between fathers' and mothers' socialization practices and children's locus of control in Brazil, the Philippines, and the United States. *The Journal of Genetic Psychology, 148* (3), 303–313.

Parrott, G. and Strongman, K. (1984). Locus of control and delinquency. *Adolescence, 19* (4), 459–471.

Powell, K. M. and Rosen, L. A. (1999). Avoidance of responsibility in conduct disordered adolescents. *Personality and Individual Differences, 37* (3), 327–340.

Rawson, H. (1992). The interrelationship of measures of manifest anxiety, self-esteem, locus of control, and depression in children with behavior problems. *Journal of Psychoeducational Assessment, 10* (3), 319–329.

Rothman, A., Salovey, P., Turvey, C., and Fishkin, S. (1993). Attributions of responsibility and persuasion: increasing mammography utilization among women over 40 with an internally oriented message. *Health Psychology, 12,* 39–47.

Shelton, T. L., Anastopoulos, A. D., and Linden, J. D. (1985). An attribution training program with learning disabled children. *Journal of Learning Disabilities, 18* (2), 261–265.

Stipek, D. J. and Weisz, J. R. (1981). Perceived personal control and academic achievement. *Review of Educational Research, 51* (1), 101–137.

Taris, T. W. and Bok, I. A. (1997). Effects of parenting style upon psychological well-being of young adults: exploring the relations among parental care, locus of control and depression. *Early Child Development and Care, 132* (1), 93–104.

Weisz, J. (1986). Contingency and control beliefs as predictors of psychotherapy outcomes among children and adolescents. *Journal of Consulting and Clinical Psychology, 54* (4), 789–795.

9. Academic Protective Factors

Boesel, D. and Fredland, E. (1999). *College for all? Is there too much emphasis on getting a 4-year college degree?* Washington, DC: U.S. Department of Education, Office of Educational Research and Improvement, National Library of Education.

College Board (2001). *Trends in student aid 2001.* New York: The College Board.

Day, J. C. and Newburger, E. C. (2002). *The big payoff: educational attainment and synthetic estimates of work-life earnings.* Current Population Reports, Special Studies, P23-210. Washington, DC: Commerce Department, Economics and Statistics Administration, Census Bureau.

Gibbs, N. (2005). Parents behaving badly. *Time,* February 21, pp. 40–49.

Institute for Higher Education Policy (1998). *Reaping the benefits: defining the public and private value of going to college. The New Millennium Project on Higher Education Costs, Pricing, and Productivity.* Washington, DC: Institute for Higher Education Policy.

MetLife (2004). *The MetLife Survey of the American Teacher;* available at http://www.metlife.com/WPSAssets/34996838801118758796V1FATS_2004.pdf.

Rowley, L. L. and Hurtado, S. (2002). *The non-monetary benefits of an undergraduate education.* University of Michigan: Center for the Study of Higher and Postsecondary Education.

Shannon, G. S. and Bylsma, P. (2003). *Nine characteristics of high-performing schools: a research-based resource for school leadership teams to assist with the school improvement process.* Olympia, WA: Office of Superintendent of Public Instruction.

Suggestions for improving reading speed. Blacksburg, VA: Division of Student Affairs, Virginia Tech.

Thompson, M. (2001). *Digest of education statistics 2001.* Washington, DC: U.S. Department of Education.

10. Personality Protective Factors

Anderson, S. and Messick, S. (1974). Social competency in young children. *Developmental Psychology, 10* (3), 282–293.

Asarnow, J. R. and Callan, J. W. (1985). Boys with peer adjustment problems. Social cognitive processes. *Journal of Consulting and Clinical Psychology, 53* (1), 80–87.

Bukowski, W. M. and Newcomb, A. F. (1984). Stability and determinants of sociometric status and friendship choice: a longitudinal perspective. *Developmental Psychology, 20* (4), 941–952.

Cassidy, J., Parke, R. D., Butkovsky, L., and Braungart, J. M. (1992). Family-peer connections: the roles of emotional expressiveness within the family and children's understanding of emotions. *Child Development, 63* (4), 603–618.

Coie, J. D., Dodge, K. A., and Coppotelli, H. (1982). Dimensions and types of social status: a cross-age perspective. *Developmental Psychology, 18* (4), 557–570.

Coie, J. D., Dodge, K. A., and Kupersmidt, J. B. (1990). Peer group behavior and social status. In S. R. Asher and J. D. Coie (Eds.), *Peer rejection in childhood.* New York: Cambridge University Press.

Denham, S. A. (1986). Social cognition, prosocial behavior, and emotion in preschoolers: contextual validation. *Child Development, 57* (2), 194–201.

Dodge, K. A., Coie, J. D., Pettit, G. S., and Price, J. M. (1990). Peer status and aggression in boys' groups: developmental and contextual analyses. *Child Development, 61* (6), 1289–1309.

Dodge, K. A., Schlundt, D. C., Schocken, I., and Delugach, J. D. (1983). Social competence and children's sociometric status: the role of peer group entry strategies. *Merrill-Palmer Quarterly, 29* (3), 309–336.

Eisenberg, N., Fabes, R. A., Miller, P. A., Fultz, J., Mathy, R. M., Shell, R., and Reno, R. R. (1989). The relations of sympathy and personal distress to prosocial behavior: a multimethod study. *Journal of Personality and Social Psychology, 57* (1), 55–66.

Fabes, R. A. and Eisenberg, N. (1992). Young children's coping with interpersonal anger. *Child Development, 63* (1), 116–128.

Franzini, L. R. (2001). Humor in therapy: the case for training therapists in its uses and risks. *Journal of General Psychology, 128* (2), 170–193.

French, D. C. and Waas, G. A. (1987). Social cognitive and behavioral characteristics of peer rejected boys. *Professional School Psychology, 2,* 103–112.

Gnepp, J. and Gould, M. E. (1985). The development of personalized inferences: understanding other people's emotional reactions in light of their prior experiences. *Child Development, 56* (6), 1455–1464.

Goldman, J. A., Corsini, D. A., and DeUrioste, R. (1980). Implications of positive and negative sociometric status for assessing the social competence of young children. *Journal of Applied Developmental Psychology, 1* (1), 209–220.

Harris, P. L., Olthof, T., Meerum Terwogt, M., and Hardman, C. E. (1987). Children's knowledge of the situations that provoke emotion. *International Journal of Behavioral Development, 10,* 319–343.

Ladd, G. W. (1983). Social networks of popular, average, and rejected children in school settings. *Merrill-Palmer Quarterly, 29* (2), 283–307.

McGhee, P. (1980). *Humor: its origin and development.* New York: W.H. Freeman & Co.

McGhee, P. (1994). *How to develop your sense of humor: an 8 step training program for learning to use humor to cope with stress.* Dubuque, IA: Kendall/Hunt.

McGhee, P. (2002). *Understanding and promoting the development of children's humor: stumble bees & pelephones.* Dubuque, IA: Kendall/Hunt.

Newcomb, A., Bukowski, W., and Pattee, L. (1993). Children's peer relations: a meta-analytic review of popular, rejected, neglected, controversial, and average sociometric status. *Psychological Bulletin, 113* (1), 99–128.

Pelusi, N. (2004). How to cultivate humor. *Psychology Today,* May 11.

Pervin, L. and John, O. (Eds.) (1999). *Handbook of personality: theory and research.* New York: Guilford.

Putallaz, M. (1983). Predicting children's sociometric status from their behavior. *Child Development, 56* (2), 253–264.

Putallaz, M. and Gottman, J. M. (1981). An interactional model for children's entry into peer groups. *Child Development, 52* (4), 986–994.

Underwood, M. K., Coie, J. D., and Herbsman, C. R. (1992). Display rules for anger and aggression in school-age children. *Child Development, 63* (2), 366–380.

11. Social Protective Factors

Agius, E. and Chircop, L. (1998). *Caring for future generations: Jewish, Christian, and Islamic perspectives.* Westport, CT: Praeger.

Blankenhorn, D. (1995). *Fatherless America: confronting our most urgent social problem.* New York: Basic Books.

Brody, G. H., Stoneman, Z., and Flor, D. (1996). Parental religiosity, family processes, and youth competence in rural, two-parent African American families. *Developmental Psychology, 32* (4), 696–706.

Brody, G. H., Stoneman, Z., Flor, D., and McCrary, C. (1994). Religion's role in organizing family relationships: family process in rural, two-parent, African-American families. *Journal of Marriage and the Family, 56* (6), 878–888.

Call, V. A. and Heaton, T. B. (1997). Religious influence on marital stability. *Journal for the Scientific Study of Religion, 36* (2), 382–392.

Carnegie, D. (1990). *How to win friends and influence people.* New York: Pocket.

Christiano, K. J. (2000). Religion and the family in modern American culture. In S. K. Houseknecht and J. G. Pankhurst (Eds.), *Family, religion, and social change in diverse societies* (pp. 43–78). New York: Oxford University Press.

Christiansen, S. L. and Palkovitz, R. (1998). Exploring Erikson's psychosocial theory of development: generativity and its relationship to paternal identity, intimacy, and involvement in childcare. *The Journal of Men's Studies, 7* (1), 133–156.

Clark, C., Worthington, E. L., and Danser, D. B. (1988). The transmission of religious beliefs and practices from parents to first-born early adolescent sons. *Journal of Marriage and Family, 50* (3), 463–472.

Cunradi, C. B., Caetano, R., and Schafer, J. (2002). Religious affiliation, denominational homogamy, and intimate partner violence among U.S. couples. *Journal for the Scientific Study of Religion, 41* (1), 139–151.

Doherty, W. J., Kouneski, E. F., and Erickson, M. F. (1998). Responsible fathering: an overview and conceptual framework. *Journal of Marriage and the Family, 60* (2), 277–292.

Dollahite, D. C. (1998). Fathering, faith, & spirituality. *The Journal of Men's Studies, 7* (1), 3–15.

Eck, D. L. (2001). *A new religious America.* San Francisco: HarperCollins.

Ellison, C. G. and Anderson, K. L. (2001). Religious involvement and domestic violence among U.S. couples. *Journal for the Scientific Study of Religion, 40* (2), 269–286.

Ellison, C. G., Bartkowski, J. P., and Anderson, K. L. (1999). Are there religious variations in domestic violence? *Journal of Family Issues, 20* (1), 87–113.

Ellison, C. G. and Levin, J. S. (1998). The religion-health connection: evidence, theory, and future directions. *Health Education and Behavior, 25* (6), 700–720.

Emmons, R. A. (1999). *The psychology of ultimate concerns: motivation and spirituality in personality.* New York: Guilford.

Fiese, B. H. and Tomcho, T. J. (2001). Finding meaning in religious practices: the relation between religious holiday rituals and marital satisfaction. *Journal of Family Psychology, 15* (4), 597–609.

Flor, D. L. and Knapp, N. F. (2001). Transmission and transaction: predicting adolescents' internalization of parental religious values. *Journal of Family Psychology, 15* (4), 627–645.

Giesbrecht, N. (1995). Parenting style and adolescent religious commitment. *Journal of Psychology and Christianity, 14* (2), 228–238.

Goldstein, A. P., Sprafkin, R. P., Gershaw, N. J., and Klein, P. (1997). *Skillstreaming the adolescent: a structured learning approach to teaching prosocial skills.* Chicago, IL: Research Press.

Lee, J. W., Rice, G. T., and Gillespie, V. B. (1997). Family worship patterns and their correlation with adolescent behavior and beliefs. *Journal for the Scientific Study of Religion, 36* (2), 372–381.

Lehrer, E. L. and Chiswick, C. U. (1993). Religion as a determinant of marital stability. *Demography, 30* (2), 385–403.

Matthews, D. A. and Larson, D. B. (1995). *The faith factor,* Vol. III. *An annotated bibliography of clinical research on spiritual subjects: enhancing life satisfaction.* Rockville, MD: National Institute for Healthcare Research.

Matthews, D. A. and Saunders, D. M. (1997). *The faith factor,* Vol. IV. *An annotated bibliography of clinical research on spiritual subjects: prevention and treatment of illness, addictions, and delinquency.* Rockville, MD: National Institute for Healthcare Research.

Pargament, K. I. (1997). *The psychology of religion and coping: theory, research, practice.* New York: Guilford.

Pearce, M., Jones, S., Schwab-Stone, M., and Ruchkin, V. (2003). The protective effects of religiousness and parent involvement on the development of conduct problems among youth exposed to violence. *Child Development, 74* (6), 420–428.

Regnerus, M. D. (2003). Linked lives, faith, and behavior: intergenerational religious influence on adolescent delinquency. *Journal for the Scientific Study of Religion, 42* (2), 189–203.

Reilly, R. (2005). Making the right calls. *Sports Illustrated,* February 8, p. 84.

Search Institute. Young people's developmental assets by involvement in religious community. Minneapolis, MN: Search Institute; see http://www.search-institute.org/congregations/faithandassetsresearch. html.

Silliker, S. A. and Quirk, J. T. (1997). The effect of extracurricular activity participation on the academic performance of male and female high students. *The School Counselor, 44* (2), 288–293.

Smith, C. (2003). Religious participation and parental moral expectations and supervision of American youth. *Reviews of Religious Research, 44* (4), 414–424.

Wills, T. A., Yaeger, A. M., and Sandy, J. M. (2003). Buffering effect of religiosity for adolescent substance use. *Psychology of Addictive Behaviors, 17* (1), 24–31.

12.   Family Protective Factors

Buss, A. and Plomin, R. (1984). *Temperament: early personality traits*. Hillsdale, NJ: Erlbaum.

Estrada, P., Arsenio, W. F., Hess, R. D., and Holloway, S. (1987). Affective quality of the mother-child relationship: longitudinal consequences for children's school-relevant cognitive functioning. *Developmental Psychology, 23* (2), 210–215.

Hess, R. D. and Holloway, S. D. (1984). Family and school as educational institutions. In R. D. Parke, R. M. Emde, H. P. McAdoo, and G. P. Sackett (Eds.), *Reviewing child development research*, Vol. 7: *The family* (pp. 179–222). Chicago: University of Chicago Press.

Mrazek, P. and Mrazek, D. (1987). Resilience in child maltreatment victims: a conceptual exploration. *Child Abuse and Neglect, 11* (2), 357–366.

Prior, M. (1992). Childhood temperament. *Journal of Child Psychology and Psychiatry, 33* (2), 249–279.

Roberts, M. and Steinberg, L. (1999). Unpacking authoritative parenting: reassuring a multidimensional construct. *Journal of Marriage and Family, 61* (3), 574–587.

Scott, W. A., Scott, R., and McCabe, M. (1991). Family relationships and children's personality: a cross-cultural, cross-source comparison. *British Journal of Social Psychology, 30* (1), 1–20.

Steinberg, L. (2001). We know some things: parent-adolescent relationships in retrospect and prospect. *Journal of Research on Adolescence, 11* (1), 1–19.

Thomas, A. and Chess, S. (1977). *Temperament and development*. New York: Brunner/Mazel.

Index

About the Author

DAVE VERHAAGEN is a licensed psychologist and a managing partner with Southeast Psychological Services. He has served as the clinical director for three mental health agencies that serve children, adolescents, and their families. He is a nationally recognized speaker and the author of five books.